#54
2⁵⁰

DISCOVERING
COMPUTERS

Cover picture: The gray square in the center of the picture is a silicon chip 9/16 inch across. The integrated circuit on which it is mounted is shown in yellow, with the connecting wires clearly visible. The entire piece has been magnified about thirty-five times.

Opposite: A silicon wafer which actually measures three inches in diameter. Each of the small squares is a silicon chip 3/16 inch across, and each contains all the circuitry needed to function as a microcomputer.

DISCOVERING
COMPUTERS
by Mark Frank

Published by

STONEHENGE

in association with

The American Museum of Natural History

The author
Mark Frank is a computer instructor, teaching new graduates the
fundamentals of computing. He graduated from Queens College,
Cambridge, in 1972, with a BA in Philosophy, and gained an MSc
in Management Science and Operations Research at Imperial
College, London, a year later. Since then he has worked
continuously in the computer industry, both as a systems engineer
helping to install and operate large computer systems and as an
instructor. Among Mark Frank's hobbies is operating his own
personal computer.

The consultant
Myron H. Goldberg is Associate Professor and Chairman of the
undergraduate and graduate Department of Computer and Information
Systems (New York campus), Pace University. He designed and
developed the BBA major in Management Information Systems at Pace.
Professor Goldberg is a consultant to the New York State Department
of Education and to industrial companies in the fields of curriculum
planning, course development, and course packaging.

The American Museum of Natural History
Stonehenge Press wishes to extend particular thanks to
Dr. Thomas D. Nicholson, Director of the Museum, and Mr. David
D. Ryus, Vice President, for their counsel and assistance in creating
this volume.

Stonehenge Press Inc.:
Publisher: John Canova
Editor: Ezra Bowen
Deputy Editor: Carolyn Tasker

Trewin Copplestone Books Ltd:
Editorial Consultant: James Clark
Managing Editor: Barbara Horn
Executive Editor: Penny Clarke

Created, designed and produced by
Trewin Copplestone Books Ltd, London

Library of Congress Card Number: 81-51991
Printed in U.S.A. by Rand McNally & Co.
First printing

ISBN 0-86706-005-0
ISBN 0-86706-057-3 (lib. bdg.)
ISBN 0-86706-026-3 (retail ed.)

Set in Monophoto Rockwell Light by
SX Composing Ltd, Rayleigh, Essex, England
Separation by Gilchrist Bros. Ltd, Leeds, England

Contents

The World of Computers

Over the next twenty years computers, more than any other invention, may well change our lives, as computers will perform ever more tasks. But most people still do not understand what computers are or what changes they will cause. This book is written for people who would like to understand how computers work and how they will develop, but have no previous knowledge of computers, mathematics or science.

Computers are becoming faster, cheaper, and smaller. An interesting way of looking at this is to compare the computer business with another industry that developed rapidly – the automobile industry, for example. Computers are developing faster than automobiles ever did. If cars had improved at the same rate as computers since 1950, a Cadillac might now cost $12, have a top speed of over a million miles per hour and run for more than 100,000 miles on a gallon of gas – and its engine would be the size of the period at the end of this sentence. This rate of change in computers is likely to continue for the foreseeable future because they are part of a new and developing technology.

When computers first appeared most people were not aware of their existence. Now computers have become so common that they are used in banks, stores, factories, warehouses, offices, and even in private homes.

Despite this, many people believe that they will never understand or be able to use computers, perhaps because they associate computers with mathematics. But in fact anyone who can add one and one together can understand enough about computers to appreciate how they work and what they are capable of doing. Computers are amazing machines, and some of the new developments in computer science surprise even the most experienced computer experts. Nevertheless, computers need not be a mystery to most people once the basis of their operation is understood. This book explains what computers are, how they work, and what they can and cannot do.

What Computers Do

Machines such as automobiles, telephones and televisions are very familiar, and most people use at least one of them every day. While computers are less familiar, they are affecting our lives just as much as other machines. But what are computers, and what do they do?

Suppose that a man keeps the scores at a track event. He receives telephone calls from the track telling him the details of competitors' performances, such as their names, numbers, and their times. It is his job to note the names of the competitors, record their positions, and display all the results on a scoreboard. This is the kind of task that a computer can do easily, and in fact computers have been used at major sporting events such as the Olympic Games for many years. In this example the scorer is taking in information by telephone, making calculations with that information and then displaying the results on the scoreboard. He is processing information, or data, and that is what computers do. Computers process data; and computer manufacturers say that they are in the data-processing industry.

Computers are not just one machine, but lots of devices connected to each other by electric cables. The data, in the form of electric signals, travels between devices along the cables. When not on the move the data is stored as an electric charge or a magnetic field.

Processing data can be thought of as taking place in stages, passing through various devices. Stage one is *input*. The data arrives at the computer from some outside source – in the case of the scorer it is a telephone call. A computer needs some way of collecting the data as input. It might be typed on a special typewriter which is connected to the rest of the computer by a telephone line.

Stage two is *storing*. The data has arrived in the computer. The scorer would probably write down the names and figures rather than try to remember them. He is storing the data before he works on it. In the same way the computer needs a place to store the data while it works on, or processes, that data.

The data would probably go straight into main storage, which is called "main" because data usually has to pass through main storage as it goes from one device to another.

Stage three is *processing*. This stage processes the data for results. The scorer would probably do this mentally; the computer makes the calculations with a device called the arithmetic/logic unit. This is so called because arithmetic and logic are its main functions. In the case of the sports event the computer compares the times of the runners (logic) and works out the order of the winners (arithmetic). The results of the calculations are passed into main storage along with the original data.

Stage four is *output*. Finally the results have to be put in some useful form. The scorer tells someone to put the names, times and the order of finish of the athletes on a scoreboard. The computer might display them on a screen similar to a television screen or print them on paper.

So each device that belongs to the computer performs something that the scorer does, although, unlike the scorer, the computer parts work with the speed of light. And there is another vital difference between the scorer and the computer. The scorer himself is capable of deciding what to do with the data, and does not need to be given instructions. All the devices that make up the computer, on the other hand, need very detailed instructions at every stage to know what to do with the data. These instructions have to be put into main storage before all the data, and these instructions are what is meant by a computer program. Every computer has to have a program in main storage before it can do anything.

This means that there has to be an extra part of the computer that reads the instructions, works out what they mean, and directs them to the appropriate device. This component is called the control unit. It is usually in the same box as the arithmetic/logic unit, and the two together are called the processing unit or processor.

The four stages of a computer processing cycle:

(1) Input – A scorer at a track event receives the names, numbers and times of the competitors by telephone; the computer receives the same information when someone types it on a typewriter like keyboard that is linked to the computer.

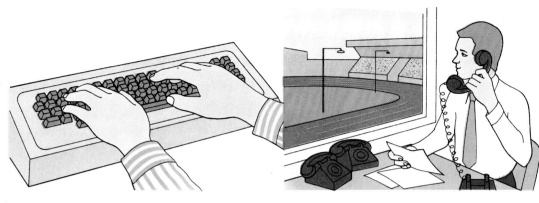

(2) Storing – The scorer writes down the information so he can refer to it while he works on it; the computer passes the information into main storage for the same reason. Main storage looks similar to a refrigerator.

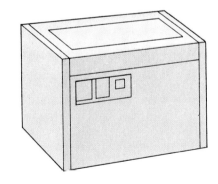 

(3) Processing – The scorer compares the times of the competitors and works out the order of finish; the computer makes the same calculation in the arithmetic/logic unit that is contained within the processor.

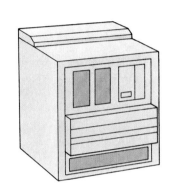 

(4) Output – The scorer tells someone to display the results on a scoreboard; the computer passes the information to an output machine called a VDU (visual display unit) that shows the results on a screen similar to a TV screen.

What Computers Are Used For

The first modern computer was in operation in 1946. By the mid-1950s a few companies were manufacturing computers commercially. The companies making these early computers each believed they would sell only about ten in the entire world. They thought computers would be used only by scientists to make long and complicated calculations. And, indeed, scientists still use computers extensively. Without the help of computers, men would never have reached the moon, for example, and flights into space would be impossible. Scientists need computers to calculate the route a spaceship will take and to make corrections in the course of the journey, among other things.

However, it did not take long for commerce and industry to catch on to the scientists' new tool, and to use computers differently. Instead of making long calculations on a few items of data – a physicist using a complicated mathematical formula, for example – they need to make a few calculations again and again on lots of data – to keep account of the different types of stock in a company's warehouse or to record the number of items delivered and dispatched.

In fact, for a long time computers were divided into two types: scientific, which were quick at doing arithmetic but did not have many input and output facilities, and commercial, which were slower at arithmetic but had more flexibility in input and output. Then in the middle of the 1960s computers became so flexible that manufacturers started to make one that was good at both kinds of work. Nowadays most computers are like this.

Computers were first used commercially to help to do jobs such as keeping a record of how much

The panel of a computer that is used to control the production of orange juice. It indicates the levels of the juice in the tanks and controls the extraction process. The lighted panel above the window shows the flow of juice throughout the factory.

The business management student is using a computer-linked visual display unit, similar to a TV screen. The computer poses questions and then flashes answers up on the screen. The student touches the answer he thinks is correct on the sensitized screen.

A computerized scanning machine takes detailed X-ray pictures of a patient, seen through a window of protective glass talking to an attendant. The screen on the operating console in the foreground displays data, while the X-ray picture is seen through the black viewer at right.

money each customer owed a company and printing the bills, or working out the shortest route for trucks delivering goods from a factory to the stores. Now, most companies have computers to do jobs such as these which would take a great deal of time if people had to do them. In fact, almost everything you buy today has been produced by an organization that relies on computers.

Computers are also used because they can react very quickly to a change of circumstance. They can physically control a process – the flow of oil in an oil refinery, for example. Electric sensing devices tell the computer the state of the process. If anything unusual happens – the amount of oil increasing or decreasing suddenly – the computer will react either by displaying a message on a screen as a warning or by sending instructions directly to some other machine, such as a valve, which alters the supply of oil so that it flows normally once more. Such a use is called a process control, and the important thing is that the computer can work fast enough to keep the process controlled.

A technician at the control board of a computer directs drilling machines that make underground pipeline tunnels. The screen and dials show the progress of the operation.

Main Storage and Bits

It is the ability to store vast amounts of information and to submit that information for fast processing that gives the computer its power. Main storage is at the heart of the computer system because a computer has to store the data and programs in main storage before the processor can work on the data. Symbols have to be used to store the data and programs in main storage. The scorer of the track and field event (pages 6–7) might store a competitor's time by writing down "21 seconds." In this case he is using eight different symbols, the digits 1 and 2, and the six letters c, d, e, n, o, s. This is typical of the method we employ to store data in written form. We use a selection from the ten digits (zero through nine), the twenty-six letters of the alphabet and other symbols such as punctuation and plus and minus signs. All the digits and all the letters are known as alphanumeric characters.

Computers, however, use only two symbols when they store data: zero and one. It is perfectly possible to use just these two symbols and record all the data needed. This is done by replacing all the characters with a code of zeros and ones, in much the same way that Morse code replaces letters and numbers with a code of dots and dashes. Computer people call zero and one "bits" (from *binary digits*, as the binary system of mathematics uses only the digits zero and one). All computers store data as bits using just these two digits to represent every letter of the alphabet and number in the decimal system.

Modern main storage consists of thousands of tiny pieces of metal that can be either full of electricity (charged) or empty of electricity (uncharged). The state of these pieces of metal is used to record data and programs. The computer designer decides either that being charged will count as the one bit and being uncharged will count as the zero bit, or the other way around. It does not matter which way. There are other storage devices besides main storage, and they also use mechanisms that can be programmed into one of two states: for example, a magnetic tape with spots that can be magnetized or unmagnetized.

When the data and program are in main storage, there has to be a means of reaching the appropriate data when it is needed. If you want to get information from a library you do not go through every shelf until you find the right book. There is normally a catalog system that directs you to the shelf where the book you want is, In the same way, computer main storage is split into locations, each of which holds one item of data and has a number called its address. The address is permanent; it is given to the location when the main storage is manufactured.

The program, once stored, will instruct the other parts of the computer system to work on the data by using the address of a location. For example, the program might instruct the input device to store an item of data at address 200. Then it might tell the processor to add the data at address 200 to the data at address 300 and put the result into address 200 in place of the original information. Finally it might tell an output device to take this new data from location 200 and print it. So a computer program has

Addresses	Bits in Locations
1	11110101
2	10111101
3	10001110
4	10101011
5	11110110
6	10110110
7	10111101
8	11010110
9	01011001
10	01110100
11	11101000

999994	10010101
999995	01111011
999996	11101110
999997	01110101

This stylized presentation of main storage shows how main storage is divided up into small areas called locations. Every location has a numbered address that is used to refer to the location. The zeros and ones within each location are the bits that represent one item of data.

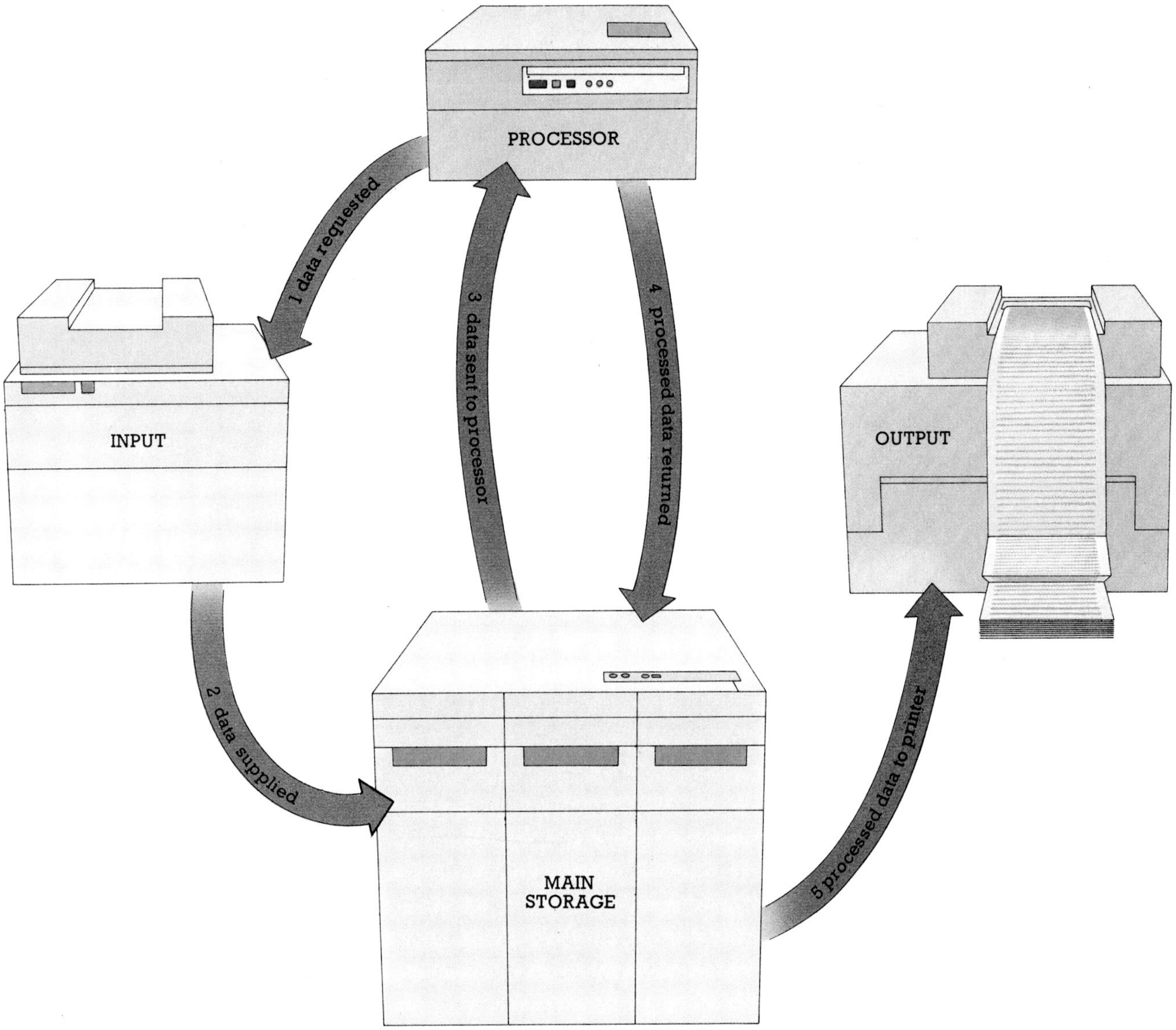
PROCESSOR
1 data requested
3 data sent to processor
4 processed data returned
INPUT
OUTPUT
2 data supplied
MAIN STORAGE
5 processed data to printer

to keep careful track of the address of each item of data. As well as the data it works on, the program itself is in main storage, so all the program's instructions will also be in locations and have addresses.

The fastest storage devices work at the same speed as the processor, so that the processor does not have to wait for information. But such storage is expensive to provide in large enough quantities. Because of this, slower and cheaper devices that back up the main storage are used for long-term storage. These devices keep the data and programs until needed, when they are transferred into main storage.

This diagram illustrates how main storage operates doing a simple computer exercise: the addition of two numbers. Once a program has been started by an operator, the processor first instructs the input machine to supply main storage with a number. On receipt, main storage sends that number to the processor along with another number already in main storage and instructs the processor to add the two numbers. The result comes back; main storage reads it in and then instructs a printer to print the result. Because all instructions and items of data must be in main storage before they can go to any other device, main storage is central to all computer operations.

The Processing Cycle

The processor and main storage form the heart of the computer. The processor, when requested, retrieves data from main store, processes it, and returns the result to main storage.

The processor and main storage consist of many parts and these must all be connected. In fact, the computer can be compared to a city whose parts are connected by roads. There are major highways, such as the one from main storage to the processor, and minor footpaths, such as those from particular locations in main storage to the major highways. The roads can be cables, wires, or microscopic pieces of metal on a silicon chip. Pulses of electrical energy, representing the bits, go along the roads.

The bits do not travel continuously, like the traffic in a town. Instead, there is an internal clock that regulates the traffic of the bits. At regular intervals it sends out an electric signal that causes all the bits that are due to travel on this signal to go to their next destination. Imagine a town in which a clock chimes every minute, and the chime is a signal for all the cars to move to the next intersection. Computers work this way, except that a modern computer will receive a signal from its clock millions of times a second. In every computer system this clock controls the basic processing cycle.

Besides the clock and the roads, there are thousands of switches, usually made from tiny components called transistors, that can be turned on or off at every signal. They are used to control which bits are read or written. For example, there are switches that are used to select locations in main storage. If the switch for a location is on, bits can travel to or from that location. If the switch is off, then the bits in that location will not be read. In the processor other transistors are connected together in groups that are used to process the data. For example, one group adds two numbers together. When the program instructs the processor to add the two numbers, the bits that represent the numbers are sent through this group of transistors. The result returned to main storage is the sum of the two numbers.

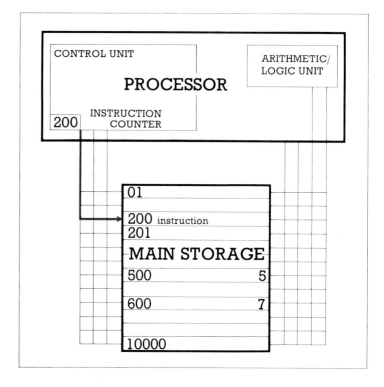

The steps in a processing cycle that adds the numbers 5 and 7 together are shown schematically in these six diagrams. (1) Select instruction. This is at address 200 as the number in the instruction counter shows.

In every computer's processor there are small storage areas called registers. They hold bits in the same way that main storage does; but they are used only for special purposes. For example, there is one called the instruction counter which is used to hold the address of the next instruction to be obeyed after the present instruction has been completed. Say a computer is carrying out a program. It has just finished performing the instruction at address 199 and now it is about to execute the instruction at address 200. This is an instruction to add the number at address 500 to the number at address 600 and put the result back in address 600. The instruction counter contains the address of the instruction to be executed, that is, 200.

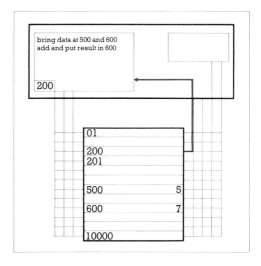

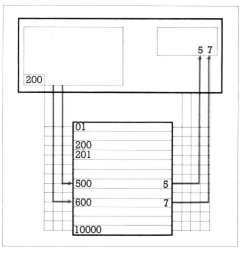

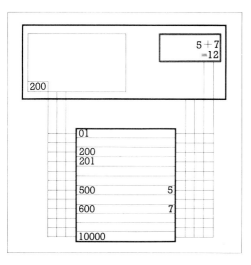

(2) Bring the instruction. The switches that give access to address 200 are opened and allow the instruction contained in the location to go to the instruction register in the control unit of the processor.

(3) Bring the data. The instruction contains the addresses of the numbers to be added together. The processor sends these addresses to main storage, *which opens the switches that allow the data in the locations to pass to the arithmetic/logic unit.*

(4) Add the numbers. A group of transistors in the arithmetic/logic unit adds the two numbers together and puts the result in a register.

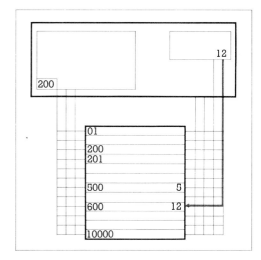

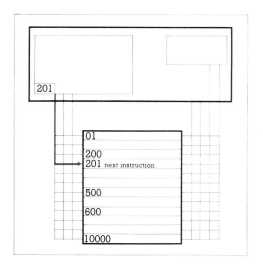

(5) Store the result. The control unit sends to main storage the address of the location in which the data is to be stored. This address opens switches that allow the data to pass from the arithmetic/logic unit into the location of that address. The data replaces the data originally in the location; the location at address 500 remains unchanged.

(6) Point to the next instruction. At the end of the cycle the instruction counter will contain the address of the next instruction to be executed, 201.

Input

Input devices are needed to get the data and the programs into main storage. They convert the data into the electric signals that the computer needs. There are different input devices, but for many years the punched-card reader was the most common.

Punched cards are so called because holes representing the data are punched into them. An operator works a keypunch machine which looks similar to a typewriter but, instead of typing letters, punches holes in the cards. After the machine has punched the holes, the cards are placed in an input device called a card reader, which is part of the computer system. The card reader converts the data that is in the form of holes into electric signals, which will then pass into storage as zero and one bits. It does this in one of two ways. One way uses small metal brushes to "feel" the holes, which are then converted by the card reader into electric currents. The more modern method shines a light onto the card as it moves through the machine and registers a current whenever the light shines through a hole. In each case, the card reader converts the data into signals and passes the signals into main storage.

A fast card reader can read and convert twenty cards a second. In computer terms this is slow, as a processor can do a million additions in that time.

The alternative to punching holes in cards is making magnetic marks on tape or disk. Both tape and disk are also used for storage.

The magnetic tape on a computer is similar to that used on tape recorders. The machines that make the magnetic marks on tape are key-to-tape machines, so called because an operator uses a keyboard to key in the data; the machine then converts the data into magnetic marks on the tape. Another device reads the data by moving the tape past an electric coil on an instrument called a read head. The coil reads the magnetic marks, and passes the data into main storage.

Alternatively, data can be keyed onto magnetic disks. These are similar in shape to long-playing records, but instead of one spiral groove there are many rings of magnetic marks on which the data is recorded. There are two types of magnetic disks: large rigid disks and small flexible ones. These flexible disks are often known as floppy disks or diskettes. They can be carried easily and even sent by mail. Both types of disks can be used for input in a similar way to magnetic tapes. The data is keyed onto a disk by one machine and then read into the computer by a different machine that moves the surface of the disk past an electric coil.

All these methods have something in common. A person has to key the data onto cards, magnetic tape, or disks before another device can read them and convert the data to electric signals inside the computer. This system can lead to errors, as people make mistakes, and it would be easier if the computer could read directly from the document on which the data was originally written. Sometimes it can. If you

This punched card carries the name "Peter Smith" and his examination mark "37." The eighty columns are numbered in small figures in the second row from top and in the bottom row. Each column of holes represents one character. The characters are printed at the top of the card so it is possible to read what the holes represent.

look at the bottom of a check you will see characters printed in odd-looking lumpy numbers. They have been printed in a special magnetic ink so they can be read not only by people but also by a magnetic character reader on the computer, which easily distinguishes the numbers by the pattern of their straight sides. There are also machines called optical character readers that can read ordinary printed documents or even handwriting.

Optical card readers are modern versions of the punched-card reader. The punched card still has rows of holes, each row representing a different character. The reader, instead of having metal brushes, has a series of photoelectric cells, each cell corresponding to a row of holes. As the card moves through the reader across these cells, a light shines down on it. Where there are holes, the light shines through and causes an electric current in the corresponding photoelectric cell. The current is turned into the bits representing the character which are then transmitted to main storage.

This keypunch operator is typing letters and numbers on the keyboard. The machine converts the letters and numbers into holes it punches in the cards.

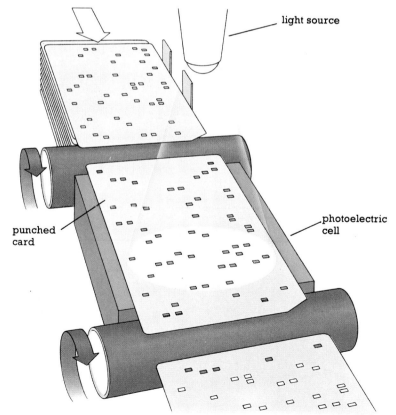

light source

photoelectric cell

punched card

An increasingly popular form of input is the floppy disk, here shown being inserted into the disk drive of a small computer system. This disk can hold 576,000 characters of data, others can hold as many as 1,100,000 characters.

15

Programs

The program is a series of instructions written to make the computer perform a task, such as working out what raw materials a factory has to buy in order to make the following month's products. At first the instructions may be written on paper by people, and then they may be stored on magnetic tape or disk, but they will eventually have to be copied into main storage, probably by another program already in main storage, before the computer can obey them.

A large program, such as the one that controlled the space shuttle, can involve a very large number of programmers for many years and cost a great deal of money. In most computer systems the programs that are instructing the computer cost more to produce than the machines themselves. What is more, the cost of the machinery is decreasing while the cost of programming is increasing as a result of labor charges. There was a time when manufacturers gave away most of their programs free with the machinery. Nowadays this is rare, and programs are bought and sold like any other product.

There are terms for all the types of products, or wares, sold by computer manufacturers. Hardware is the physical machinery in a computer system, which includes processors, disk drives, main storage, card readers, magnetic tapes and magnetic disks. Software denotes the programs that go with it.

Software is as important as hardware, and the boundary between the two is not as sharp as it might seem. There is a middle road, called firmware. In this case the processor is built to obey only a few simple instructions, such as moving a bit from one location to another. Then the manufacturer writes a program that uses these simple instructions to perform more complex instructions, such as dividing one number into another. This firmware is a part-program that is in the machine all the time, and forms the basis of all subsequent programs.

The computer is said to be a programmable device, and without a program it cannot work. There is no such thing as a computer that does not need a program.

Computers are not the only programmable mach-

In this upright Steinway player piano, made in 1910, the roll of programmed paper can be seen in the center in pink. The player piano was patented in 1879 by E. H. Leveaux of Surrey, England.

ines, however. In 1852 a Frenchman named Martin Corteuile patented an organ that was programmable. Holes punched in a card determined the tune it played. This was an early programmable device to use a punched card as the program input.

Since then there have been many programmable devices, and the computer is only one of them. A famous example is the player piano or pianola, a programmable piano. The program is created by playing a tune on the keyboard, and as the tune is played the player piano punches a hole for each note in a roll of paper. The same roll of paper can then be used to control the player piano so it plays back the tune without the keyboard being touched.

These rectangular holes in a player piano's roll of programmed paper are read by small levers. These levers start the mechanism that causes the keys of the piano to play. A different roll of paper will produce a different tune.

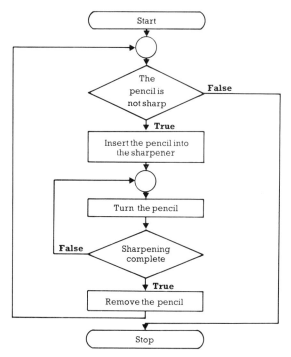

A series of instructions for an imaginary program to sharpen a pencil would look like this. If the pencil were already sharp the program would branch to STOP. If the sharpening were not complete, the program would branch back and repeat itself.

Operating Systems

In a modern computer system there is one special program that is brought into main storage before any other programs are loaded. This special program remains accessible until the computer is switched off. It tells the computer to read into main storage the first ordinary program, to start working on it, and, when it has finished, to read in the next ordinary program, and so on. A special program has lots of names. It can be called an executive program (it is similar to an executive of a large company, as it is in charge of and organizes other programs and allocates the computer's resources), a supervisory program, a control program, or an operating system. In this book the phrase "operating system" is used. The operating system shares main storage with the other programs that come and go. Its job is to make all the other programs work.

Suppose a computer program has been written to calculate how much commission each salesman in a company should be paid, based on the number of items he or she has sold. We can call it a commissions program. Suppose, too, it has been stored on a magnetic disk.

The commissions program cannot be used by the computer unless it is in main storage, so the program has to be copied from disk into main storage before the computer can begin work. The program can be read in from a disk in the same way as ordinary data, but the relevant part of the operating system must be already in main storage to tell the computer to read in the commissions program when it is needed. Since the operating system is itself a program, the computer must have a means of reading it into main storage when the machine is switched on. The computer often has a special button to control this process which may be called "initial program load."

Besides loading other programs into main storage, the operating system can do many other useful things. With a good operating system, for example, it should not be necessary for anyone to be near the computer while it runs its programs, except for emergencies and simple jobs, such as putting more paper in the printer when it runs out. A good operating system will even check that it is working on the correct data by making sure that it is using the correct magnetic tape for any particular program.

Locations
0

Operating
System

50,000

Ordinary
Program

70,000

Unused
Capacity

100,000

A diagrammatic representation of the 100,000 locations of a typical small computer's main storage would look like this. The operating system, which controls all the programs in main storage, occupies locations 1 through 50,000 and stays in them all the time. Locations 50,001 through 70,000 are taken up by the program currently being performed, leaving locations 70,001 through 100,000 unused in this particular example. These locations are empty, but they could contain bits. In that case although the data represented by the bits is unused, the bits will not be removed until a fresh program is entered that overwrites them. In the example illustrated, a new program read in will be able to occupy any of the locations 50,001 through 100,000, overwriting the existing program.

XYZ Inc. Monthly Report on Years of Service

NAME	AGE	YEARS OF SERVICE
Adams P.	10	300
Albricht R.	33	210
Appleyard S. T.	121	010
Austin K. A.	15	000
Balson C.	23	995
Bell W.	9	911
Blowry F. L.	98	020
Bright D.	18	340
Byewell R. L.	27	040
Carson S. P.	23	780
Castle P. R.	24	380
Cattlington U.	55	040
Close B. C.	35	234
Cobbler H.	29	020
Costwell T. R.	15	456
Cooper R. M.	18	230
Cooper T.	42	566
Cusper H.	38	291
David J.	24	391
Davies R.	84	635
Davis J.	26	665
Dawson P. L.	43	021
Deadwell N.	21	040
Debbing S.	31	934
Delacroix P.	19	201
Dickson V. A.	51	041
Dill G.	31	035

This printout shows the sort of error that a good operating system can help to prevent by detecting human or machine errors. The computer was asked to produce a list of a company's employees with their ages and years of service. But the program used as input a tape that contained the employees' salaries instead of their ages and years of service. Adams has a salary of $10,300 and so the program has taken the first two digits as his age and the second three as his years of service. Had the operating system checked the identity of the tape, it would have alerted the operator that the wrong tape was mounted.

Sometimes an operating system also helps if the ordinary program goes wrong. At the very least it will print a report on what went wrong, and it may be able to help correct the error or find a way around it. Operating systems usually control several programs at the same time. For example, one program may be receiving its input, a second program may be processing input, and a third program may be printing its output.

Operating systems are normally supplied by the manufacturer with the rest of the system, and they are just as important as the hardware. They are like the supervisors in a factory – they do not actually produce the goods, but they help the people who do.

Instructions

A computer can do complicated tasks only because a program has been written which combines simple instructions. Even the most complicated computers can recognize only a few hundred instructions – surprisingly – and a simple computer system might recognize only the instructions to do the following:

1. Read data from an input device to main storage.
2. Write data from main storage to an output device.
3. Move data from one address in main storage to another.
4. Change the values of particular bits from zero to one or vice versa. (This is sometimes necessary because a single bit may be used to represent a fact, such as whether or not a person is married; if an unwed employee gets married, then it would be necessary to change that bit.)
5. Add, subtract, multiply, and divide numbers.
6. Branch to other instructions.
7. Stop.

Typically, the instructions might be combined thus – two reads, one add, one write, and one stop – to make a simple, five step program that reads two numbers from an input device such as a punched-card readers, adds them together, and writes the result on an output device such as a printer. These instructions are enough to process two items of data as illustrated in the diagram on the opposite page.

Even simple instructions for a computer program are difficult to write and even understand. They are in main storage in the form of bits. For example, the pattern of bits 1111101000000000000000011111010-00000001001011000 looks very complicated. But it is in fact an instruction for one particular processor to add the data in location 500 to the data in location 600 and put the result in location 600 as the diagram (below) shows.

However, even though computers are limited in the range of instructions they can follow, and despite the fact that their programs are difficult to write, computers have the advantage of speed and accuracy. An average processor can add two numbers in a millionth of a second. That means it could add a column of typewritten numbers two and a half miles long in a second. Furthermore, a computer properly programmed would get the answer exactly right. It is almost impossible to imagine a person adding up so many numbers and always getting the correct answer. What is more, the newest processors can perform twenty million additions a second, and the maximum speed increases every year as better computers are developed.

All this speed is useful only because a computer can operate without human help for a long time once it has the instructions to do so. If you use a pocket calculator you have to keep on keying instructions into it until you have finished your calculations (unless it is programmable, in which case it is really a small computer). You cannot tell it to work out a complicated sum, such as how much fuel an airplane will need to fly the Atlantic, and go away to let it do the work. You can do this with a computer once it has been programmed. The instructions are placed in main storage beforehand so you do not have to supply them while the computer does the calculation.

This is the sequence of bits for the instruction described in the text (above right). The bits would be in a continuous stream; they are divided into sections here to show which bits apply to the different parts of the instruction.	**11111010**	**00000000**	**0000000111110100**	**0000001001011000**
	Add	**This indicates the number of digits in the numbers to be added**	**The address of the first of the two numbers to be added. Here it is 500**	**The address of the second of the two numbers to be added together. It is also the address where the result is to go. Here it is 600**

Two punched cards, one with the number five punched on it, the other with the number seven, are put in the card reader and read into main storage. An instruction in the program in main storage tells the processor to add the two numbers together. The total, twelve, goes back into main storage and then to the printer. A real program would contain hundreds of instructions and do much more complicated operations on many numbers – such as taking the ages of all the people in a census, working out how many there are of each age, calculating the average age.

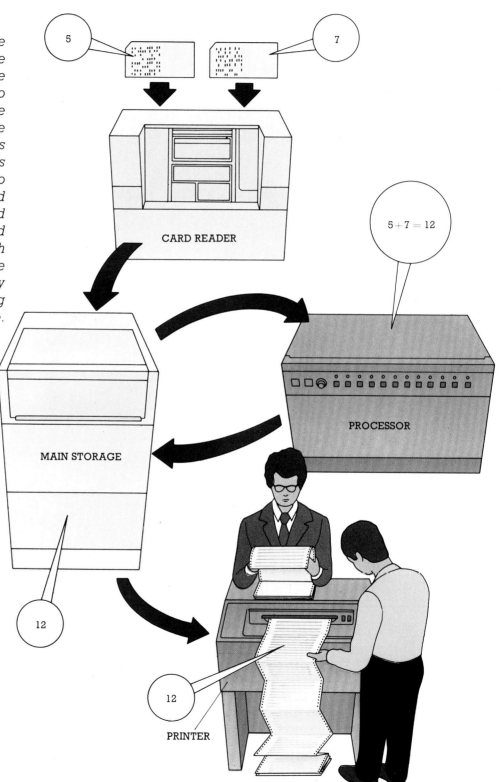

5

7

CARD READER

$5 + 7 = 12$

PROCESSOR

MAIN STORAGE

12

12

PRINTER

Branch Instructions

Once a processor has read one instruction from the program in main storage the instruction counter will normally give the computer the address of the following instruction. A typical sequence of five instructions to add two numbers together and print the result might be in consecutive locations in main storage starting at address 198 and ending at address 202. If the instruction in location 202 is not "stop," as it is in diagram 1, the computer will perform the instruction there and then continue to the instruction in location 203.

With such a program in main storage the computer would obey each instruction in the program once and once only. When the control unit encounters a branch instruction in the program, however, the computer will not go on to execute the next instruction in the sequence but will branch to another one somewhere else in main storage. This happens because the instruction counter has altered to point to some completely different location. The computer will start executing instructions at this new location and will not go back to the instruction after the branch unless instructed to do so by a further branch instruction.

Branch instructions also make it possible to repeat a group of instructions very often. To do this the last instruction in the group is a branch instruction that takes the computer back to the first instruction in the group. A group of instructions which repeats itself like this is called a loop.

The five instructions in diagram 2 are a loop as the last instruction in location 202 is not "stop" but "branch to location 198." This group of instructions would continue reading numbers from the input device, adding them together and printing them out until the computer was switched off. Thus somehow the loop must be stopped when the work is completed and the computer is required to do something else.

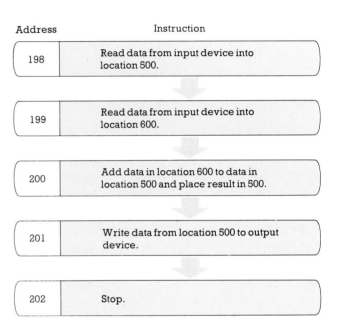

Address	Instruction
198	Read data from input device into location 500.
199	Read data from input device into location 600.
200	Add data in location 600 to data in location 500 and place result in 500.
201	Write data from location 500 to output device.
202	Stop.

(1) Sequential programming – These instructions are in consecutive locations in main storage, starting at address 198. Once the instruction counter has been set to 198 all the instructions would be executed automatically.

For this reason, besides instructions that branch every time they are performed, there are also instructions that cause a branch only if some condition stated in the program is fulfilled. For example, if in diagram 2 we know that none of the numbers being read into location 500 are zero, then the program can be written so that it branches out of the loop when all the pairs of numbers have been read in and added together. This is done by putting a dummy pair of numbers at the end of the list, of which at least the number read into location 500 is zero. As shown in diagram 3, the two numbers are added together and the result put into location 500. As the number read in to location 500 was zero, the numbers now in locations 500 and 600 must be

Address	Instruction
198	Read data from input device into location 500.
199	Read data from input device into location 600.
200	Add data in location 600 to data in location 500 and place result in 500.
201	Write data from location 500 to output device.
202	Branch to location 198.

(2) Infinite loop – A group of instructions such as this would go on adding two numbers together indefinitely. The instruction at address 202 causes the processor to branch back to the instruction at address 198.

Address	Instruction
198	Read data from input device into location 500.
199	Read data from input device into location 600.
200	Add data in location 600 to data in location 500 and place result in 500.
201	Write data from location 500 to output device.
202	Branch to location 198 if contents of location 500 do not equal contents of location 600.
203	The rest of the program....

(3) Conditional branch instruction – This group of instructions continues adding two numbers together until it meets two zeros, which are added like preceding numbers. The result tells the computer to go on to the rest of the program.

equal. Because of this, the loop will not take place and the program will continue with the instruction at location 203.

In this example the computer branched whenever the two numbers compared were not equal. However, branch instructions may also be devised and used to branch on all sorts of other conditions, for example when two numbers are equal, when a number in a main storage location equals zero, or when a number is greater or less than a given number.

A branch instruction need not always point back. It might equally well transfer the flow of instructions to an entirely different part of main storage. For example, suppose a program to calculate students'

examination results occupies locations 800 to 850 in main storage. Locations 851 to 899 contain the instructions that process the data about the students who have passed – those who have obtained more than or exactly fifty per cent. Locations 900 to 949 contain the instructions that process the data about the students who have failed by receiving less than fifty per cent. Location 850 could then have the instruction that says ''if the student's mark is less than fifty per cent, branch to the instruction in location 900.''

Computer Languages

As we know, when programs are in main storage ready for execution they are represented by a series of bits; in this form they are said to be in machine language.

The very first programs were written in machine language – the programmers worked out the instructions in bits and then wrote down those bits.

```
01001000  00010001
00110000  10111000
10100111  00111001
00001000  11110010
```

Each of these four lines of bits is one instruction in a computer program. The lines have been broken in the diagram to make them easier to read.

This took a long time, it was easy to make mistakes as there were so many zeros and ones to write down, and mistakes were difficult to correct. Even worse, if another programmer took over a program and had to alter it, he or she found it almost impossible to understand what had already been written.

For these reasons programmers developed other languages in which to write programs. These languages are the same throughout the world, whatever the spoken language. Programmers write in these special languages, and the computer itself will then translate them into machine language. A very famous example of these languages is COBOL, much of which looks like English. It is not English, though, and there are very strict rules in using it. For example, you could not write "transfer" instead of "move" as the computer would not recognize the word. Even so, COBOL is much easier to write, correct, and under-

```
MULTIPLY TOTAL BY 2 GIVING NEW—TOT.
MOVE NEW—TOT TO OUTPUT.
WRITE OUTPUT.
```

These three statements in COBOL would multiply the number in the location called TOTAL by two and then print the result. Some of the words, such as MOVE and MULTIPLY, mean what they say. Other words, such as TOTAL and OUTPUT, are names chosen by the person writing the program to represent locations in main storage which represent data.

```
RREAL = −B/(2.0*A)
DISC = B**2−4.0*A*C
RIMAG = SQRT (ABS(DISC) )/(2.0*A)
IF (DISC .LT. 0.0) GOTO 500
    R1 = RREAL + RIMAG
    R2 = RREAL − RIMAG
    WRITE (6,301) R1, R2
    GOTO 100
    WRITE OUTPUT 'NO REAL ROOTS'
    GOTO 100
```

This is part of a FORTRAN program that is intended to solve a mathematical problem: for example finding the real roots of a quadratic equation. FORTRAN and other computer languages are now accepted by many graduate schools as a substitute for foreign languages as a condition of entry.

stand than bits, and a programmer will finish writing a program more quickly using COBOL rather than machine language.

COBOL is a good language if the computer is to be

used for a business application, such as working out a company's inventory (in fact, it stands for *CO*mmon *B*usiness *O*riented *L*anguage). It is the most widely used computer language in the world.

There are many other languages that are designed for other uses. FORTRAN (*FOR*mula *TRAN*slation), for example, is a language designed for scientists, and BASIC (*B*eginners' *A*ll-purpose *S*ymbolic *I*nstruction *C*ode) is a simple one designed so it can be learned easily.

COBOL, FORTRAN, BASIC and newer languages are called high-level languages because they express the program in the way in which the programmer expresses his or her solution to the problem. Low-level languages express the same solution in a form that may be directly used to control the computer and its associated devices. Each statement in a high-level language program must be translated into a low-level language before it can be executed by the computer. When translated, each high-level language instruction will usually produce many low-level or machine-language instructions. As a result, the program may take more time to run, or it may occupy more main storage than if it had been written in machine-language.

If a program is to be very efficient it should be written in a low-level language, but since each statement represents only one instruction a low-level language takes longer to write and is more difficult to change. Because, of this, low-level languages are written only for computer programs that are to be used frequently and not changed very much.

A user wants a language that has been designed for his or her uses. FORTRAN is particularly popular for scientific work, because with it one can write complicated scientific formulas quickly and easily. A low-level language is not designed for any particular application, and it is difficult to use for writing both scientific formulas and business reports. How-

```
A    14, 15
ST   R1, OUTPUT
L    R2, NEXTNO
B    12
```

Each line of this part of a low-level language produces one instruction in the form of bits when it is translated. The "A14, 15" in the top line means "add the data in the locations at addresses 14 and 15." "B12" in the bottom line means "branch to address address 12."

ever, a low-level language allows the programmer to manipulate the parts of the computer exactly as desired. For example, a low-level language can specify exactly how many locations of main storage are to be used to store a certain item of data, whereas a high-level language would give the programmer no choice, and might use a larger amount than was needed. In order to take advantage of this facility of low-level languages, the programmers using them have to know a great deal about the computer, and this is certainly true of the programmers who work for computer manufacturers.

BASIC

BASIC is one of the simplest computer languages and so is particularly suitable for writing programs at a terminal for immediate execution. Suppose a person wants to use BASIC to work out the number of seconds in a year, that is, $60 \times 60 \times 24 \times 365$. The picture below shows what the program might look like. The answer, 31,536,000, would be displayed on the terminal at which it was entered.

This example is typical of the way arithmetic is presented in BASIC, and indeed in many other computer languages. Numbers, such as 365, are written in decimal in the ordinary way. The operations that are to be performed on the numbers are written mostly using well-known symbols: $+$ for addition, $-$ for subtraction, and / for division. However, the $\times$ multiplication symbol can be confused with the letter x, so, in common with many other languages, BASIC uses * for multiplication.

The equals sign can be used in BASIC in the same way as it is in arithmetic, but it can also be used in another way, depending on the instruction. In our example the equals sign instructs the computer to pass the value of $60 \times 60 \times 24 \times 365$ to location X shown in line 10.

The letter X is a label for the location chosen by the programmer to store the results of calculations. Any letter or suitable sequence of a letter and a digit could have been used. All computer languages allow programmers to refer to storage locations with a label.

Line 20, the second line of the program, takes the information at the location referred to by X and prints it at the terminal. It also would be possible to get input from the terminal by using a line such as "80 input X" which would instruct the machine to read a number from the terminal and put it in the location which has the label X.

The final line is "end." This instruction tells the computer to stop running the program.

There are many other BASIC instructions which are not included in this example, of course. Two which should be mentioned are typical of most computer languages: the "if" and loop control instructions.

It is possible for the program to make a decision using an "if" instruction. This is so called because if a statement is true the computer will obey the instruction; if untrue the computer will carry on with the rest of the program. This is illustrated on the page opposite in the left hand diagram which shows a short program that reads two numbers from the terminal and divides the first by the second.

Most computer languages have a way to repeat a

```
10  LET X = 60 * 60 * 24 * 365
20  PRINT X
30  END
```

Each line of the program begins with a number (10, 20 or 30 in this example). The numbers may increase by any value greater than one to allow extra lines to be inserted if necessary. Line 10 makes the calculation. Line 20 displays the result.

```
10   INPUT X1, X2
20   IF X2 = 0 GOTO 50
30   LET R = X1/X2
40   PRINT R
50   END
```

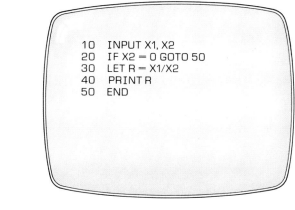

```
110  ....
120  LET X = 0
130  FOR I = 1 TO 100
140  INPUT Y
150  LET X = X + Y
160  NEXT Y
170  ....
```

An example of a BASIC program which uses the "if" instruction. The first line shows the input of the two numbers to locations X1 and X2. The "if" instruction in line 20 checks that the second number is not zero as it is impossible to divide by zero. If the second number, referred to as X2, is zero the computer goes to line 50, that is "ends." If X2 is not equal to zero, the computer continues with the division shown at line 30 and prints the result.

This is part of a larger program that reads in a hundred numbers from the terminal and adds them to each other, one at a time. Lines 140 and 150 are the ones being repeated. Each number is read into location Y, and the processor passes the result of each addition back into location X in main storage. If the first five numbers were 6, 4, 11, 11 and 5, the process would be $0+6 = 6, 6+4 = 10, 10+11 = 21, 21+11 = 32, 32+5 = 37$, and so on until all one hundred numbers were added together.
The "for" and "next" instructions on lines 130 and 160 are parts of the instruction that defines the loop. The "for" says that all the lines until "next" are to be repeated and the value in location I is to be increased by one each time. This will continue until the value in location I reaches one hundred; then the program will proceed to line 170.

group of instructions many times in a loop as the right-hand diagram above shows.

With the few instructions shown here it is possible to write programs that read numbers from the terminal, do quite complicated arithmetic, and display the results at the terminal. BASIC can be learned quickly and as a result it is very popular among people who are not computer specialists but who want to write their own programs.

Translating Computer Languages

A computer cannot obey a program until it is translated into machine language, but the computer itself can be instructed to make the translation.

Imagine you have written a program in a high-level language – COBOL, for example – which is going to read in the names of all the students at a large high school, sort them into alphabetical order and then print them in that order. Such a program could be called a ''sorting'' program. You would write the sorting program in the form of COBOL statements on paper. Next, you would key the statements onto punched cards or magnetic tapes or disks. These statements are said to be the source program, because they are the source from which the computer will make the translation from COBOL into the bits of machine language.

The computer now uses the source program as data for another program, the compiler. The compiler is generally written by the computer manufacturer and supplied with the computer; it is brought

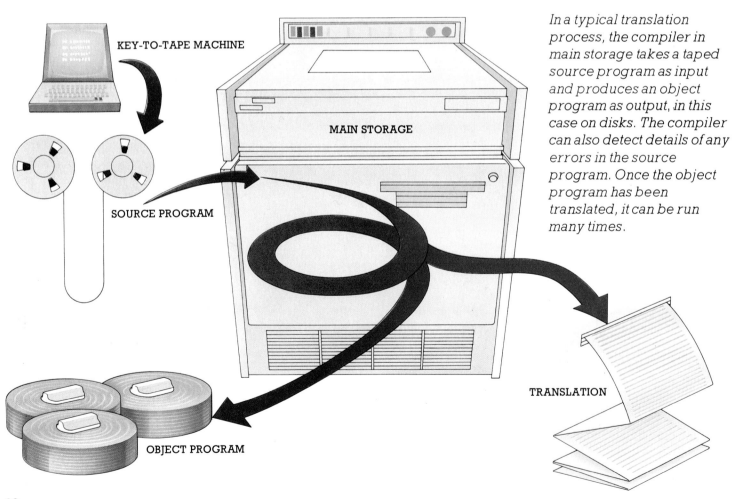

KEY-TO-TAPE MACHINE

SOURCE PROGRAM

MAIN STORAGE

OBJECT PROGRAM

TRANSLATION

In a typical translation process, the compiler in main storage takes a taped source program as input and produces an object program as output, in this case on disks. The compiler can also detect details of any errors in the source program. Once the object program has been translated, it can be run many times.

into main storage in machine language. The compiler now takes the COBOL sorting program as data and then produces the machine language version of it. This machine language form of the program is often called the object form. The object form is stored on magnetic disks or tapes. Often the only printed output from the compiler is a statement that the computer has received the program. Now that the compiler has translated the sorting program into a language the computer can understand and obey – the object form – the computer can carry out the program. The compiler itself does not obey the instructions of the sorting program. It simply produces a version of it in the machine language that the computer can use. The sorting program itself must still be carried out.

Besides providing an object form, most translating programs will detect any errors in the source program. In this case the computer will print details of the errors as printed output, along with the statement that it has received the program. For example, in a COBOL program the programmer might accidentally write "moove" instead of "move." The compiler finds that it does not know how to translate this word into bits. There is no point in translating the rest of the program without that statement, so the compiler prints that it is unable to make the translation, giving details of why it cannot do so. Some of the most modern compilers will guess what the incorrect word was meant to be and substitute this guess for the error so the translation can be completed. But the compiler will still print a warning.

Compilers are very effective when they are used conversationally. The programmer enters the source program at a VDU or some other terminal and the compiler then reads the source statements and translates them into machine language. If the compiler finds any mistakes it will display them on the VDU screen so they can be corrected immediately. This is a very fast way to produce a program the computer can work on.

The very first compilers were in machine language because otherwise the computers could never have obeyed them. Nowadays, though, computer manufacturers write compilers in a high- or low-level language. The manufacturers then run the compilers on a computer that is programmed to translate the high- or low-level language into machine language. This machine language version is then fed into the individual computers that the manufacturer will sell.

Part of a printout of a COBOL program, which the compiler was trying to translate. The programmer made a mistake in line 2700, writing "TOO" instead of "TO." The compiler therefore printed two messages because it did not recognise the word "TOO," and could not find the word "TO" that it expected. As a result the compiler was unable to translate the program. The numbers at left and right are the program's sequence numbers. "NCOUNT" is a word the programmer has chosen just for this program.

002600	STEP-2.	READ FILE-1.	00002600
002700		MOVE RECORD-1 TOO RECORD-2.	00002700
002800		WRITE RECORD-2.	00002800
002900		ADD 1 TO NCOUNT	00002900
003000	STEP-3.	PERFORM STEP-2 UNTIL NCOUNT IS EQUAL TO 5.	00003000
003100	STEP-4.	CLOSE FILE-1.	00003100
003200		CLOSE FILE-2.	00003200
003300		STOP RUN.	00003300

CARD	ERROR MESSAGE	
002700	IKF30011-E	TOO NOT DEFINED
002700	IKF40071-C	TO MISSING OR MISPLACED IN MOVE STATEMENT.

Magnetic Tapes

Even small computer systems generally have to store very many millions of characters, and a large system, such as a bank's, will store trillions of characters of data. The capacity of main storage would need to be enormous – and the machines therefore costly to build – if all this information were stored in main storage, so there has to be some form of back-up storage as well. Magnetic tape is used for back-up storage besides being a popular form of input.

A program in main storage instructs a tape drive to read and write the data on the magnetic tape. A read/write head on the tape drive both writes data onto the tape and reads data from the tape. To write the data, the read/write head, which is electromagnetic, makes magnetic marks on the tape, each mark representing a bit of data. As it writes, the head simultaneously erases any information previously stored on the tape (although some manufacturers produce tape drives with separate erase heads to do this). When the read/write head reads the data, the head converts the magnetized areas it "sees" on the tape and transmits them as bits to the computer.

The magnetic marks are in parallel lines, called tracks, on the tape. Most tapes have six or eight tracks of data, with each track made up of bits that align in rows with corresponding bits on the other tracks. Each row of six or eight tracks normally represents one character. A seventh or ninth track on these tapes contains bits that, instead of recording data, check that the bits on the other tracks are correct. A typical full-length reel of tape can hold over a hundred million characters of data.

An important aspect of magnetic tape is how close the bits are to each other along the track. The closer together the bits are, the more data there is on the tape. Moreover, the closer the bits the faster the computer can read them. This phenomenon, called density, ultimately determines the storage capacity of a tape. At the moment the fastest tapes have more than 6000 bits per inch of track and the computer

Magnetic tapes mounted on two tape drives. Each tape drive has a takeup reel fixed permanently on the left-hand side. The tape to be read is placed on the right-hand side. A plastic ring (here it is a red one) is placed at the center of the tape to allow the computer to write on the tape. When the ring is removed, as on the tape at the right, the read/write head can only read from the tape. This is a way of preventing the data on the tape from being overwritten accidentally.

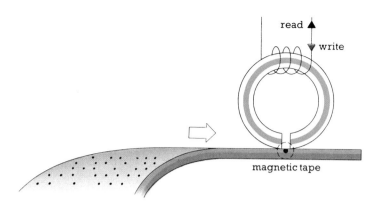

A read/write head on a tape drive both reads and writes the bits on magnetic tape – though not simultaneously. A bit is created by passing a current, shown in red, through the head and this magnetizes a small area of the tape which represents a bit. The head can also read (shown in black). There is one read/write head for each track of data on a tape, and there are typically eight tracks of data with a ninth track which checks that the other eight are correct.

The size of the gap can be reduced, and the tape made to perform more quickly, if the tape drive accelerates and decelerates very fast. Computer tape drives use motors that have a faster acceleration than almost any other machine made. From being stationary they can reach two hundred inches a second in less than a thousandth of a second. If they carried on at that acceleration for a whole second they would be traveling at twice the speed of sound!

However, magnetic tapes have one great disadvantage: the computer has to search through the tape in sequence until it reaches the appropriate data. Despite their speed this can take up to a minute or so if the data is located in the middle of the tape. This makes them unsuitable for certain applications, such as those in which the computer has to answer questions very quickly – telephone inquiries personnel using computer-linked screens to look up telephone numbers, for example.

can read the data at over a million characters a second. A fast tape drive could read this book in less than one second.

There is a problem, though. The computer cannot read a whole magnetic tape in one continuous running because it would not be able to fit it all into main storage. For this reason, the data on a tape is broken up into shorter pieces, called blocks. The tape has to stop between blocks while the processor works on the preceding one. If the tape stops, it needs some time to slow down and more time to accelerate again before it reaches the next block. But the tape drive cannot read data while the tape is speeding up and slowing down since it has to travel at a constant speed. This means there is a length of tape between blocks which is not used for recording data but only for accelerating and decelerating. It is called the inter-block gap.

This operator is placing a reel of magnetic tape on one of the five drives shown. The lights indicate what the tape drive is doing – whether it is reading from the tape, waiting for instructions from the computer, or whether the tape is simply being rewound.

Magnetic Disks

Magnetic disks have one great advantage over magnetic tapes: speed of access. The computer can reach each item of data stored on disk almost immediately. This is important when the computer has to respond very quickly – for example, to an airline reservations clerk asking the computer if there is a spare seat on an airplane. In fact, without the speed of magnetic disks many of the uses of computers would be impossible.

Magnetic disks vary from about eight to thirty-five inches in diameter. Usually, several disks are stacked one on top of the other on a common central spindle to form what is known as a disk pack. The whole pack revolves on a machine called a disk drive at about three thousand revolutions per minute – about

The operator above is about to remove a disk pack from the drawer of a disk drive, of which there are four in this installation. The drawer must be closed before the disk drive can be started.

The tracks on a disk compared to the lines on a human thumbprint. The tracks are represented as parallel lines to demonstrate how many there are, but disk tracks are not actually visible, as they consist of magnetic marks.

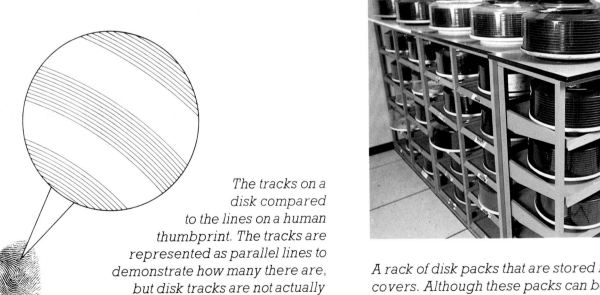

A rack of disk packs that are stored in protective covers. Although these packs can be removed from the disk drives, other packs are permanently mounted on the machines.

There are five disks on this simplified disk pack (twenty disks are more common). The access arm moves the read/write heads back and forth between the disks, reading or writing the data on the upper and lower surfaces. The upper surface of the top disk, and the lower surface of the bottom, are usually not used.

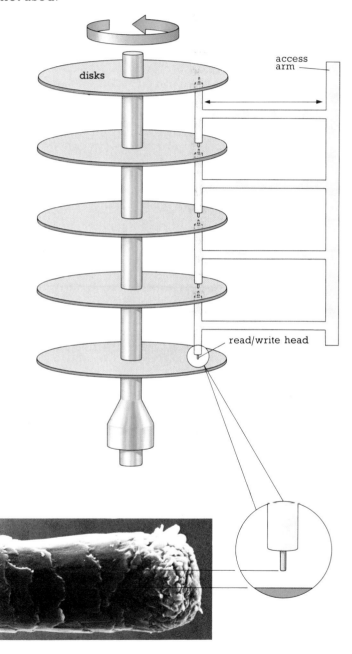

disks

access arm

read/write head

The diameter of a human hair, here magnified about 800 times, is greater than the gap between a read/write head and the surface of a disk.

one hundred times the speed of a long-playing record.

The disk drive has an access arm that moves between each set of parallel disk surfaces. This access arm is branched, and at each end of the branch is a read/write head – one for the upper disk surface, one for the lower. Each head both reads and writes all the magnetic marks that represent the data. The heads shoot to and fro, reading or writing while the disk drive revolves, although they do not actually touch the surfaces of the disks.

The number of magnetic marks that can be put on every hundredth of an inch of track is one of the most important qualities of disk, because the more magnetic marks there are, the greater the amount of information that can be stored and the faster the computer can read that information. A deciding factor in how close together the marks can be to each other is how close the heads can get to the surfaces of the disk. The closer the heads are, the more easily they can tell where one mark ends and another begins. At the moment the heads float on a cushion of air very close to the surface – about a few millionths of an inch away from the surface. If the proportions were enlarged so that the head were the size of a jumbo jet, the plane would be flying at less than a tenth of an inch above the level of the ground.

The newest types of heads actually rest on the surface of the disk when the disk drive is stationary. As the disk starts to revolve the head takes off and floats on its cushion of air ready to read or write the data. Of course, the computer has to know the address of the data, which it finds by reading into main storage from the disk an index that lists which disk and which track have the relevant data. When an airline booking clerk inquires about a flight, for example, the computer looks at the index and moves the head for a certain disk to the appropriate track – in this case the details of flight 420 are on track ten of disk three. Reaching the track takes a fraction of a second. Then the computer waits for one revolution at the most until the correct data is under the head. At this point the computer transfers the data into main storage. If the data had been on magnetic tape, the computer might have needed to rewind the whole tape, leaving the clerk and customer waiting while it did so.

Codes

To get the words and numbers of programs and data properly onto computers each character has to be coded with the same quantity of bits. This is because it is very difficult to design groups of transistors – in physical terms the electronic components on silicon chips – which can process data that has a variable number of bits per character. The codes, however, vary between computers.

number of bits		number of characters
1	(0 or 1)	2
2	(00 to 11)	4
3	(000 to 111)	8
4	(0000 to 1111)	16
5	(00000 to 11111)	32
6	(000000 to 111111)	64
7	(0000000 to 1111111)	128
8	(00000000 to 11111111)	256

The designer of the computer decides how many bits the computer will use to represent each character. The fewer bits used, the less main storage each character takes up. However, if too few bits are used it is not possible to represent enough different characters.

The characters PETER SMITH would be coded like this in main storage using EBCDIC. Each letter occupies eight bits – one byte – and so does the blank space between the two words. The computer will give an address to each byte. When an instruction refers to the name PETER SMITH, it will need to know the address of the first byte (150) and the length of the name (11 bytes).

Suppose we want to store the name PETER SMITH in main storage. We would type PETER SMITH into an input device, such as a keyboard with a TV screen attached. The device would then convert the letters to bits in main storage, in the code for the letters "P," "E," "T," etc. But how many bits are needed to code one character? If we tried to use two bits per character there would be only four possible combinations: 00, 01, 10 and 11 – which is not nearly enough.

Early computers used six bits for each character, but it is now most common to use eight bits employing a code such as the Extended Binary Code Decimal Interchange Code (EBCDIC). By using eight bits for each character, a total of 256 characters can be coded with the variations of eight zeros and eight ones. Computer people call a group of eight bits a "byte" (pronounced *bite*).

Main storage, as we have seen, is divided up into locations, each with a numbered address. A common practice is for each location to be large enough to store one character, so that every byte in main storage has an address. When the processor wants to refer to some data it asks for the data beginning with a certain byte number, which depends on where the data is stored.

That is how data such as names and telephone numbers are stored in main storage. This kind of information is called character data, which means any data that is *not* going to be used for arithmetic (a number such as a telephone number counts as character data). Numbers that are used for arithmetic are called numeric data. Numbers are usually coded in a different way from character data because arith-

150	151	152	153
11010111	11000101	11100011	11000101
P	E	T	E

154	155	156	157
11011001	01000000	11100010	11010100
R	space	S	M

158	159	160	
11001001	11100011	11001000	
I	T	H	

character	code
A	11000001
B	11000010
C	11000011
⋮ Z	⋮ 11101001
a	10000001
b	10000010
c	10000011
⋮ z	⋮ 10101001
0	11110000
1	11110001
⋮ 9	⋮ 11111001
space	01000000
$	01011011

This code uses eight bits for each character. It can represent all the capitals and small letters, the ten digits, and a large number of mathematical symbols, punctuation marks, etc. Notice there is a code – 01000000 – to represent a blank space.

metic instructions such as adding would need many complicated groups of transistors if numbers were coded as character data.

Suppose a computer has to calculate how much Peter Smith earned in a week. It would need the number of hours Peter Smith worked, together with the amount he was to be paid per hour. These figures must be multiplied: they are numeric data which has to be coded differently from the letters of his name.

Numbers in our common decimal system can either be written in the form of words – twenty-eight – or by using the ten digits – 28. The binary system does not use the ten digits of the decimal system but uses only zero and one to represent all ten digits. Twenty-eight is written as 11100 in the binary system, for example.

With the binary system the largest number that one byte can hold is 255, which comprises 256 numbers (zero through 255). This would not be much use for the computers that worked out the route for the Apollo moon landings, for example, so most computers

employ a larger group of bits for holding numbers in the binary system. This group is called a "word."

The size of a word varies from one computer to another. A common size for large computers is thirty-two bits, which can hold all the numbers up to 4,294,967,295. Some of the large computers that are especially suitable for scientific work have sixty bits in a word, and this code will hold numbers up to a quintillion (one followed by eighteen zeros in ordinary decimal numbers). But scientists often want computers to make calculations that use even bigger

number	divided by	result	remainder
109	2	54	1
54	2	27	0
27	2	13	1
13	2	6	1
6	2	3	0
3	2	1	1
1	2	0	1

To convert decimal numbers to binary, the decimal number is divided repeatedly by two until the final result is zero. The remainders from the divisions become part of the binary number. By using this principle, the decimal number 109, above, is converted to 1101101 in binary, reading the remainder column from bottom to top.

numbers. In these cases the numbers are too big for the word-size in the binary system and another, more complicated, code is used with which it is possible to represent numbers of almost any size.

Computers that have one byte for every address in main storage are called byte-oriented computers. The computers that have one word for every address in main storage are called word-oriented computers, and they are often used for programs that do a great deal of calculation.

Printing

The results of all computer programs are given in some form of output. They may be displayed on a screen like a TV screen or in the form of punched cards to feed into another computer. Often the information has to be printed so that people can easily read and understand it. Printing machines have to change the data from electricity in main storage to print. They do this by converting the bits that arrive from main storage into the characters represented by the bits, and printing those characters.

Computer printing is very fast, although printing machines, being mechanical, do not nearly equal the speed of an average processor, which can make a million additions each second. An adapted electric typewriter can be used for computer printing, but this is too slow for printing a lot of data because it prints only one character at a time. Most computer printers in fact print a whole line of type at a time. Some of these models can print two thousand lines in a minute, which means they could print all the words in this book in about three minutes.

The most popular computer printer is called simply a line printer. On a typical line printer the characters are similar in size to those of an ordinary typewriter, and two thousand of them pass a print position every second. The hammer which hits the paper against each character has to do this quickly so that the printing is not blurred. The machine makes such a clatter that it is usually the noisiest in the computer room. The speed and the detailed mechanism involved suggest that line printers may easily break down, but they are very reliable and they have been one of the most common means of printing output since the beginning of the 1960s.

Two thousand lines a minute sounds fast, but it is still slow compared with the speed of the processing unit. Unfortunately, line printers cannot go much faster because they have moving parts, which are bound to be slow compared with the electronic speeds of the processor. As a result, faster printers have been developed, and these use mechanical movement only to pull the paper through the machine, not for the printing itself. One kind of printer burns

Line printers print on an unbroken sheet of paper called a continuous form that folds itself at the back of the machine. Each fold is perforated so that it can be torn easily to separate the forms into pages.

the letters onto the paper (a laser printer); another kind squirts drops of ink, which have been charged with electricity, at the paper (an ink-jet printer). The drops pass through an electric field which directs them to the shape to form letters or digits.

The fastest printers of all work like photocopiers. They create a pattern of an electric charge on a drum inside the printer (a laser beam can do this too). The electric charge attracts a type of black dust, that is already in the machine, to the drum, and this dust is transferred from the drum to the paper as printing. These printers can print 20,000 lines a minute! And they have a lot of other advantages besides speed. A line printer can print only the characters that are on the chain, whereas this electrical printer changes characters simply by laying down a different electric charge, so it can print completely different types of characters (*italic* and **bold**, for example) on the same page. Such machines can even draw pictures and graphs, and they print much more clearly and neatly than do the more usual printing machines.

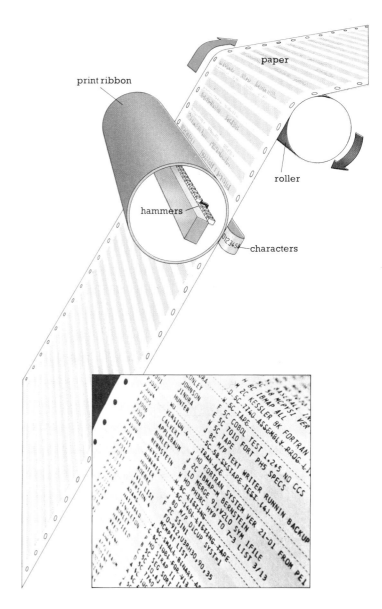

Here a laser beam is being directed by a computer, a principle used in some high-speed printers, in which the laser draws the patterns of the letters on the paper. Lasers, being electronic, can print very much more quickly than line printers, whose speeds are limited because they operate mechanically.

The diagram of the mechanism of a line printer shown above has all the characters on a chain that revolves behind the paper several times a second. When the appropriate characters reach the correct positions, hammers bang the print ribbon against the paper, which hits the characters. The most common characters, such as "e" and "o," are repeated many times on the chain so that the hammer does not have to wait for the character.

Inset is an example of printed output. The rollers of the line printer use the holes, seen in this close-up only on the left side of the sheet, to move the paper through the machine.

A Computer in Action

While companies use computers to perform a great variety of tasks, a common usage is to calculate how much pay a company's employees are to receive at the end of each week. Imagine that company XYZ, Inc., uses its computer to do this.

Before the computer can do the calculation, the data has to be collected. In this case the computer needs two kinds of data: the data about all the employees that ordinarily does not change from one week to another – their names, how much they are paid per hour, and so on – and the data that may change from week to week – the number of hours each employee has worked that particular week. The data that does not change every week is kept permanently on a magnetic disk pack, which is known as DATAPK. The first track of DATAPK contains an index that says on which track of which disk in the pack are the details of each employee.

The data that changes from week to week is on punched cards. As each employee arrives and leaves the building he or she inserts his or her own card into a punching machine that is attached to a clock. The machine punches holes in the cards which indicate the times the employees started and finished work each day that week. Each week the cards are collected and taken to the computer room.

The computer room houses a small commercial installation – a processor, main storage, several disk drives, a card reader, and a line printer. The computer operator puts the cards into the card reader so that it can read them when the operator starts the machine. He places on the disk drives two disk packs – DATAPK and another disk pack, called PROGPK, which contains the program that makes the calculations. An operating system is already in main storage and this copies the program from PROGPK into main storage, although the original copy remains intact on the disk. The operating system sets the program counter so that it contains the address in main storage of the first instruction in the PROGPK program. The processor then starts to execute the program.

The first thing the program does is to tell the disk drive to read into main storage the index on the first track of DATAPK. Then the program tells the card reader to read the data about the employee on the first card, whereupon the program copies into main storage the name and the number of hours he or she has worked. The program tells the processor to look at the name and work out from the index where on DATAPK the details about the employee will be. Given this information, the program tells the disk drive to read the DATAPK details about the employee into main storage.

Once this is done all the data on this employee is in main storage. Now the program can tell the processor to work out how many hours the employee worked each day and then for the full week (from the data originally on the punched cards) and multiply by the amount he or she is paid per hour (from the data originally on the DATAPK disk). Then the program tells the printer to print a line giving the employee's name, the number of hours he or she has worked and the amount he or she is to be paid. Now the program branches back to the instructions that tell the card reader to read the next card. The program then repeats the cycle with that card, and so on. Finally, when the PROGPK program detects it has read all the cards and printed the results, it tells the processor to stop.

The whole process will take only a few minutes. The time taken for the calculation is negligible. The limiting factors are the time needed for the card reader to read the cards and for the printer to print the lines. The permanent data on DATAPK will remain on the disk, as will the program on PROGPK. There is also now a copy of the program in main storage, but this will simply be overwritten by the next program that is run.

A computer system like this one may take less than two minutes to calculate the pay of all five hundred employees in a company using only two of the available disk drives, one card reader, main storage, one processor, and a printer.

MAIN STORAGE & PROCESSORS

TAPE DRIVES

OPERATING CONSOLE

CARD READER

DISK DRIVES

Computer People

Many people imagine that computers are machines that operate independently of human intervention. Even more common is the belief that those people who work with computers must be mathematicians or scientists. In fact, all computers depend on people, most of whom certainly need not be mathematicians or scientists. Some of the more common jobs connected with computers are mentioned here. And an important point is that all jobs in the computer industry can be conducted equally well by men or women: whenever "he" is mentioned "she" is meant as well.

A computer is always part of a wider system that involves machines and people other than the computer and its operators. In fact, data processing might be a small part of the entire system. Take the example of a computer that produces the final stock market quotations at the end of a day. It is part of a system that starts with the opening price of the stock each day, and finishes with the closing price and the total number of shares traded. The computer, which monitors these steps and generates the final tabulation, is only a small part of the overall picture.

The person who identifies the elements needed in a system and the steps required in using it is the systems analyst. He spends a lot of time talking to the people who will use the system: the brokers, the customers, the computer staff, the people who handle the money, and so on. The systems analyst builds into his final design the needs and requirements of each of these people. Later he produces a detailed description of the system, including all the data that will go in and out, the devices necessary to handle it, and the programs that will have to be written. This description is then passed to the application programmer.

An application programmer writes the programs that the computer needs to do some task, such as calculating the total number of shares traded. However, he does not spend all his time writing programs. His work overlaps with the analyst's, as the descriptions of what the programs have to do may not be clear (in fact some people do both jobs simultaneously). He also has to plan the programs before they are written, and he spends as much time testing, correcting, and changing programs as he does writing them in the first place. It is common to think of the computer programmer as someone who talks to no one and spends all his time using the computer. He must have a logical mind, certainly, but it is just as important for an application programmer to be able to get on with all the other people with whom he works.

Another person involved with computers is the systems programmer. He does not write programs for particular applications, but instead looks after the entire computer system. It is his job to ensure that the computer system provides a good service to all its users, including the application programmers. He spends a lot of time working out how to make the computer fast, reliable, and easy to use. He may also advise other users and try to solve any problems they may have. To do this he needs to be an expert both on the machines and the programs that make up the computer installation.

Once the program has been designed, it may be coded for the computer by a keypunch operator who can add or change data as it becomes available.

It is the computer operator who works in the computer room and pushes the buttons that start and stop the computer. His tasks vary from simple jobs such as removing paper from printers to vital and complicated ones – for example restarting the program if something goes wrong. The operator has to be able to act quickly to rectify any fault because otherwise the people using the computer will be kept waiting.

A small computer system such as this may have two or three keypunch operators, two or three systems programmers, five or six application programmers, and two systems analysts. The number of personnel varies greatly and depends on what the company uses the computer for.

41

Computers in the Home

Computers have become so inexpensive that they are now a popular hobby. You can buy one for less than $200, and if you are prepared to wire together some of the components yourself you can get a kit even cheaper than that.

A typical home computer includes a processor, main storage, a keyboard for entering data and programs, and a connection to an ordinary television, which acts as a visual display unit (VDU). There is often some way of reading from and writing to a cassette tape. The tape can be used to store programs and data, and is a handy way of passing programs to other people. Usually, part of the main storage has a simple operating system written into it permanently; this is the read only memory (ROM), which prevents data already in the computer from being overwritten. The ROM also contains a program that will translate input into bits. This means that people can write their own programs in a simple computer language, generally in BASIC.

Many people buy home computers for the sheer fun of programming them. There is a great thrill in getting the computer to do exactly what you want. For example, if you are preparing for an examination of some sort you might program it to test you – it will never get tired or bored. In the course of writing the programs you will learn a lot about computer programming, a skill very valuable in itself and which may be as important in the future as knowing how to drive a car.

The small keyboard in the foreground is a computer that is compact enough to be used at home. It attaches to an ordinary television set, which acts as its visual display unit, or VDU.

The computer game plugged into the television (left) is teaching grammar. It is asking which part of the sentence "I looked through the window" is a pronoun. The other games are "Speak & Spell" (shown above foreground) and "Speak & Read," which teach by spelling and pronouncing words.

Another popular use of home computers is to play games. The games available at the moment need to be plugged into ordinary television sets, and they simulate anything from tennis to a space war. The advantage of having your own computer is that you can not only buy games that have been programmed in advance but also write your own programs and invent new games.

A home computer can also be used in very practical ways. You can use it as a super diary, for example. As with an ordinary diary you would type in important dates, such as birthdays and holidays. Then you could program the computer so that whenever you switch it on it reminds you of any important events that are coming up and continues to remind you until you have done something about it (and told the computer that you have done so). You could also include regular events that you do not want to miss, such as a favorite television program. You enter the time and day of the week and the computer reminds you every time the program is due.

Some people connect their home computer to other electrical equipment in the house. It can be used to switch things on and off automatically. For example, this feature can be used to discourage burglars. While the house is empty it switches lights, television

sets, and other electrical equipment on and off in just the same way as if the house were occupied.

If you are prepared to spend more money you can buy a printer. It can allow you to use the computer for preparing all kinds of written material: letters, essays, invitations, and anything that you would normally write on paper. Instead of writing a letter you could type it into the computer. Once it is stored there you can add to it, alter it, copy it – whatever you like – far more easily than if it had been on paper. Then, when you are happy with the finished product, you can print off as many copies as you want, and you can have one or two phrases different on each copy. If you belong to a club or society you could keep the names and addresses of all the members on the computer. Whenever you want to send a letter to all of them you type just one letter and the computer prints a copy for each member and inserts the name and address in the appropriate places.

It is difficult to write a program to do all this yourself, but there are programs for sale which do just this kind of thing. There are also clubs and magazines for home computer enthusiasts. Owning your own computer is fun. You do not need to know about electronics to use one, all you need is a desire to find out more about computers.

Conversational Computers

Computers can be used in two main ways. The first to be developed was that in which a computer works on a problem more or less by itself. For example, if someone wants a computer to calculate a company's monthly stationery requirements and print a listing of those requirements, the operator puts the program in the computer, puts the data in the correct input device, and can then leave the machine. The operator can come back later and, provided nothing has gone wrong, the printed output should be waiting for him.

The other use is completely different. In this approach the computer does not work on the problem all by itself, it has a conversation with the user, and this is called a conversational, or interactive, application. One of the best examples of this is the use of a computer to make reservations for seats on airplanes. If you go to an airline ticket office and buy a ticket for a seat on a plane, the clerk will probably have a machine consisting of a small television-type screen attached to a keyboard like that on a typewriter. This machine is connected to a central computer, which might be on the other side of the world. The clerk will query the computer by typing onto the keyboard questions such as which seats are still free and how much they cost. The

Visual display units are usually monochrome, but color VDUs are becoming more and more common. The output is normally in the form of characters, but it can also be a diagram or graph, as in this case.

computer will flash the answers on the screen. When you have bought the ticket the clerk will tell the computer that your seat is now reserved.

Obviously, someone who wants a conversation with a computer needs a device that does both input and output, as he or she needs to talk to the computer with input, and the computer has to talk back with output. These devices are called terminals, and they can be very simple. The typewriter kind is probably the simplest. The operator types messages on the keyboard, which are printed onto paper in the ordinary way; these messages are also sent as input to the computer. The computer replies by working the keyboard itself and printing the answers at the terminal. Typewriters used to be the most common kind of terminal, but nowadays most people use a device like the one used by the airline clerk: a screen plus a keyboard. The input is keyed in and is dis-

To obtain cash from a cash-dispensing terminal at a bank, the customer follows these instructions:

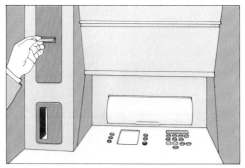

1. Insert card into terminal

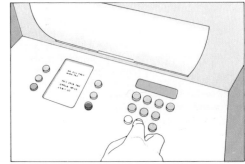

2. Key in personal number

played on the screen: the computer displays its answers, the output, on the screen too. This type of terminal has lots of names. The screen part has a cathode ray tube like a television's, so it is often called a CRT or just a tube. It is also called a VDU – the term used in this book.

Typewriters and VDUs are general-purpose terminals. They can be used for all sorts of things, from finding the latest prices of grain quoted by the commodity exchange to entering orders at a factory. It all depends on the program. Other terminals are especially designed for a particular application and are used by people who may not even realize that the machines are computer terminals. The cash-dispensing machines at banks, for example, are computer terminals. When a customer uses one, the computer tells the terminal to discharge cash as a form of output if there is enough money in the account; it also deducts the amount from the customer's account.

Conversational computing began as an unusual way of using computers. Twenty-five years ago the main point of computers seemed to be to make long calculations or to handle masses of data very quickly. But during the last five years the conversational applications came to dominate the others.

3. Tell the terminal cash is required

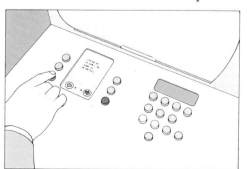

4. Key in the amount

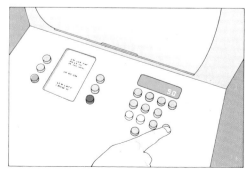

5. Remove money

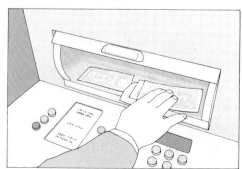

Transistors and Chips

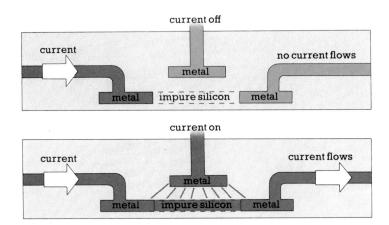

Electric switches are essential parts of any computer. They are different from ordinary light switches in several ways. One of the most important differences is that an electric current turns them on and off, not the movement of someone's hand. Electric impulses in the computer, such as those carried by other transistors or the pulses from the clock, can turn them on and off millions of times a second without human intervention. Computer switches are also considerably smaller than ordinary light switches, and in fact they cannot be seen with the naked eye.

The first computer switches were made from various components, such as electronic valves, but they would be too slow, too unreliable, and above all too expensive for the computers in use today. Luckily, at about the same time that computers were invented transistors were also invented. They were used as a much better and cheaper kind of switch. Transistors make the modern computer possible.

To understand how they work, consider that an electric current can be compared to water flowing along a pipe. The electric current is analogous to the amount of water that is flowing, and the voltage at any point is like the water pressure at that point. A transistor acts as a faucet in the middle of the pipe, to turn the water on and off. The two states of the transistor switch – on and off – represent the two bits, zero and one, or vice versa.

The first transistors were made individually, but now they are mass produced using the famous silicon chip. A chip consists of thousands of microscopic transistors manufactured within a piece of silicon that is often so small it will go through the eye of a needle.

These diagrams show the principles behind one of the commonest types of transistor: two pieces of metal are placed on each side of an impure silicon semiconductor with a third piece of metal slightly above. When no voltage is applied, the transistor is off and the semiconductor does not conduct (top). However, when voltage is applied the semiconductor becomes a conductor and an electric current flows through the transistor.

Transistors are made of silicon because it is what we call a semiconductor. Some materials, such as metals, carry, or conduct, electricity very easily. These materials are called conductors. Other materials, such as rubber, do not conduct electricity; these are insulators. Silicon is halfway between a conductor and an insulator. Hence it is known as a semiconductor. Pure silicon does not conduct electricity at all. But if very small quantities of certain impurities, such as metals, are added it can conduct electricity under some conditions. As soon as the electric current is removed the impure silicon will no longer be able to conduct. The current switches the transistors on and off very quickly, and this is why computers are so fast.

A chip consists mostly of pure silicon, but a little impurity is added to it wherever a transistor is needed and a means provided to apply a voltage very close to the impurity. Channels of pure metal connect the transistors to each other and to the rest of the system. The transistors and the connecting channels are so small that it is now technically possible to get 450,000 transistors on a chip about a fifth of an inch square. By 1990 computer experts expect there to be one million transistors per chip.

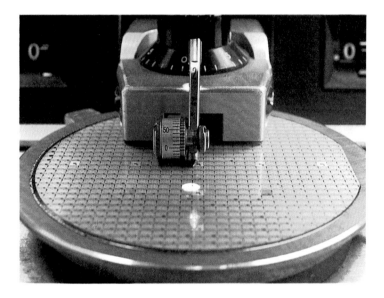

These microscopic transistors and the connecting channels are put on the chip by a process called photolithography. The chip is covered with a chemical called a photoresist. Then a fine pattern of ultraviolet light is shone on it. The ultraviolet light hardens the photoresist on the chip, making it difficult to wash off. The photoresist not exposed by the ultraviolet light, on the other hand, washes off easily. After the chip has been washed it is covered with the metal and other impurities that make the transistors and connecting channels. These impurities stick only to the places where the photoresist was washed off. Finally, the hardened photoresist is removed with a solvent, leaving only the metal and impurities needed in the desired pattern. This process is repeated many times with the impurities to build up layers of transistors and channels on the chip. It can be applied to hundreds of chips at once, although a large proportion of the chips will be thrown away because there is no way of repairing them if any of the connections are faulty.

Transistors are used throughout the computer system. There are transistors in main storage which may allow bits to pass to the processor if the transistors are switched on. There are other switches in the processor which are connected together in groups. These groups change the data, by adding data together, for example.

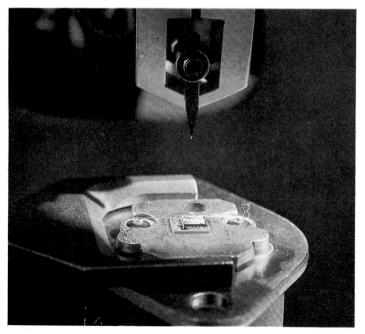

Chips are manufactured in batches on a wafer of silicon (top). After manufacture, the wafer is checked by a machine that sends a tiny probe to touch each chip to test the circuits. The probe marks any faulty chips with a spot of red paint. Once the chips have been tested, a diamond-tipped saw (center) cuts the wafer into individual chips. Gold wires, which will link the chips to the rest of the computer, are then soldered onto a chip (left).

Storage Chips

The chips in main storage contain transistors, but they also usually contain other electronic components, including some called capacitors.

A capacitor is simply a place on the chip where electricity collects when a voltage is applied. If an electric current is like water flowing along a pipe and the voltage is the water pressure, a capacitor is like a very strong rubber balloon attached to one end of the pipe. The higher the pressure, the more water is stored in the balloon. Reduced pressure means the water leaves the balloon and flows back into the pipe. The same principle is true of a capacitor. When a voltage is applied, electricity flows into the capacitor until it is full and the current stops; if the voltage is removed the current flows the other way and the electricity leaves the capacitor.

A storage chip is a collection of thousands of these capacitors. When full of electricity any capacitor will count as a one bit, when empty as a zero bit (or vice versa). Thus the capacitors hold the data in main storage as electric charges or non-charges. Each capacitor is connected to a metal conductor which can carry electricity between the capacitor and the rest of the computer. Transistors act as simple switches between the capacitors and conductors. Most of the time the transistors are closed to keep in whatever electricity is in the capacitor. Only when a capacitor is being written to, or read from, is its transistor opened.

Whenever the processor sends an address to a main storage chip it opens the transistors for the locations at those addresses, and the information becomes available as an impulse, or not, from the capacitor. If the processor is reading data from main storage, then the electricity flows along the conductors to the processor. If the processor is storing data then it sends electricity along the conductors and it is then stored in the appropriate capacitors.

However, the capacitors release their data when the processor reads from them, and thus lose their electric charges. Because of this, whenever the processor reads data, the data has to be written back again immediately. The electrical circuits to do this are usually on the chip, so the processor does not do it. In fact, the capacitors lose their electricity even when they are not being read, for they gradually leak. If the chips were left alone all the data would disappear in a fraction of a second, so all the data has to be read and written back again at regular intervals. A typical interval is two thousandths of a second. Again, the circuits to do this are usually on the chip, so a storage chip is a hive of activity even when the

A capacitor stores up an electric charge when an electric current is applied to it in the same way that a rubber balloon might store up water. Before the charge is applied it is as if the balloon were empty (1); the faucet is turned on and the balloon fills with water (2). A transistor can be turned off at the entrance to the capacitor; this is like switching off the faucet once the balloon is full (3). If the transistor is turned on again the electricity will escape (4).

(1)

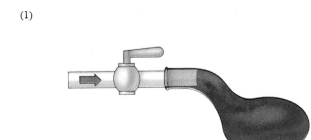

(2)

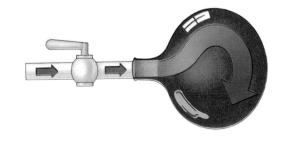

This storage chip (above), held in someone's fingertips, is 1/5 inch square. It can hold 64,000 bits — enough for 8000 characters.

Wires have been soldered to this chip so it can be connected to other circuits. The chip itself is the small square at the center.

processor is not actually making any use of it.

This kind of storage chip is called random access memory (RAM for short). RAM chips comprise the most common kind of computer main storage, although there are many other types. One is ROM. In this case the bits are put into the chips by the manufacturer and they cannot be changed.

While the process of putting storage bits on chips gets cheaper each year through technological progress, chips are the most expensive part of main storage. And although manufacturers are continuing to put more and more bits on chips as the process becomes cheaper, they can encounter some peculiar problems. One such problem is cosmic-ray particles. These are minute particles of radiation, smaller than an atom, that come largely from outer space and are always present in the atmosphere. People never normally notice these particles, but a capacitor is so tiny that it can fail to function properly if a particle hits it. As a result, computers in the future may need a special covering made from very dense material that the particles cannot penetrate. Even now, some computers cannot be used above a certain altitude without special protection, because the greater the height the more particles there are.

(3)

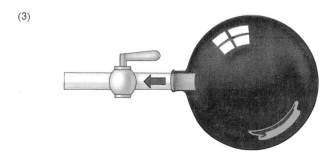

(4)

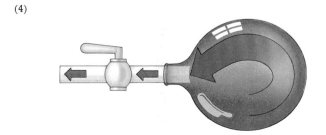

Processing Chips

In a processor the data goes through a sequence of switches that will change the data, by adding some numbers together, for example. Some bits will arrive at the processor from main storage – in this case the bits that represent two numbers. And the chips in the processor must return a different set of bits to main storage – the bits that represent the sum of the two numbers. While they are being processed the bits are stored temporarily in areas on the chips called registers.

Every different instruction that the processor performs will lead the data through a different sequence of transistors, each of which may change the data in a different way. There will be one sequence of switches for addition, another for multiplication, and so on. The sequence consists of taking the data through one or more groups of switches that perform part of the instruction. For example, nearly every computer has a group of switches which can add two numbers together. Such a group is called an adder.

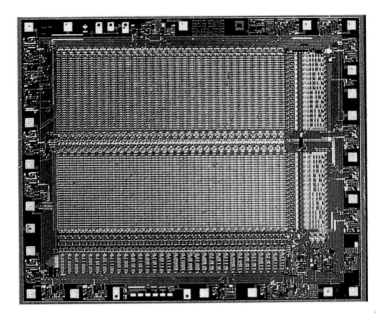

This chip contains thousands of transistors and connecting circuits which are used to process data. There are places, called registers, where the bits are stored temporarily while they are being processed, and sets of switches that work on the data, such as adders that add some bits together.

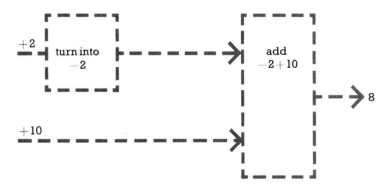

A group of switches that add can also be used for subtraction. Here, an instruction to subtract two from ten leads the two through an adder group of switches that turns the two into its negative value. The adder then adds ten to the value which gives the right result.

This group can also be used to perform subtraction, multiplication and division. The add instruction will send data directly to the adder in the processor, which sends the result back to main storage. For example, suppose the instruction is to add the numbers 1 and 2. The number 1 is represented by bits 01, and 2 by 10. The adder will change the bits into 11, which represent the number 3. A more complicated instruction, such as subtraction (as illustrated at left), might first lead the data through another group of switches and then use the adder before returning the results to main storage. An instruction to multiply might use the adder many times in the course of one multiplication. In each case the processor still only follows one instruction from main storage; and that one instruction causes the data to go through a particular sequence of switches.

An adder may involve hundreds of switches, and there are many different designs. However, computer manufacturers make all large groups on a processing chip, such as adders, by combining a large number of small groups that do very simple changes to just one or two bits. These small groups are often called gates. There are only a few types of gate, but they are sufficient to build whatever complicated group is desired. For example, it is possible to make a gate called a not gate out of just two switches. A not gate does the very simple operation of turning a one bit into a zero bit and vice versa. That is why it is called a not gate – the bit that comes out is not the bit that went in. By itself a not gate is useless. But any operation such as addition involves changing a zero bit to a one bit and vice versa. So once a designer has made a not gate he can connect it to other, similar simple gates to produce a more complicated group, such as an adder.

There is a mathematical system, called Boolean algebra, that shows how to connect simple groups to

Two transistors on a silicon chip which measures 6 × 4 mm. The chip is the dark rectangle, the transistors are the lighter areas on it and the pale background is the ceramic substrate in which the chip is embedded. The fine gold wires are the connections between the transistors. Although this chip holds only two transistors, chips of a similar size can hold tens of thousands.

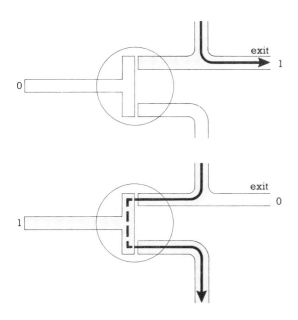

Diagram to show how a not gate uses a transistor to change a zero bit to a one bit and vice versa. Top: low voltage (representing a zero bit) is applied at left to the transistor within the circle. The low voltage switches the transistor off. The current, which is always applied at the top, flows out to the right, causing high voltage representing a one bit. Bottom: high voltage representing a one bit is applied at the left. This turns on the transistor, which allows the current to flow out at the bottom, where it is not used. No current escapes to the right, which represents a zero bit.

make complicated ones. One of the conclusions of Boolean algebra is that for any operation needed it is possible to design a group of switches to do it. As a result, it is theoretically possible to put any instruction on a computer provided enough switches are used. However, the number of switches, and therefore transistors, that are needed increases enormously as operations get more complicated.

This is one reason why some computers are much more powerful than others. Although a simple computer may be able to add two numbers almost as quickly as a more sophisticated one, it has very few groups of transistors and they can do only very simple operations. The result is that such a computer contains only the gates for a few basic instructions, such as additions of whole numbers (never fractions). The programs for a simple computer therefore need more instructions written into them because the programs have to use the gates repeatedly to perform complicated tasks. A more sophisticated computer will have more groups of transistors, so it has the gates to perform a greater number of different instructions, such as adding numbers with fractions. As a result it can do the same task with fewer instructions written into its programs.

Microcomputers and Microprocessors

Computers have been getting smaller since they were first invented primarily because it has become possible to get more and more transistors onto a chip. The 1960s saw the introduction of mini-computers – small, cheap computers that usually perform only one task at a time. In the 1970s an even smaller and cheaper computer was developed – the microcomputer, one of the most dramatic results of silicon chip technology.

A large computer's circuits are divided among a number of chips. There are several for the processor, several for main storage, and probably one or more for controlling the various input and output devices attached. However, we have now reached the stage where it is possible to put all the electronics for a simple computer on one chip. A chip that has a complete processor on it is called a microprocessor. If main storage and input and output control facilities

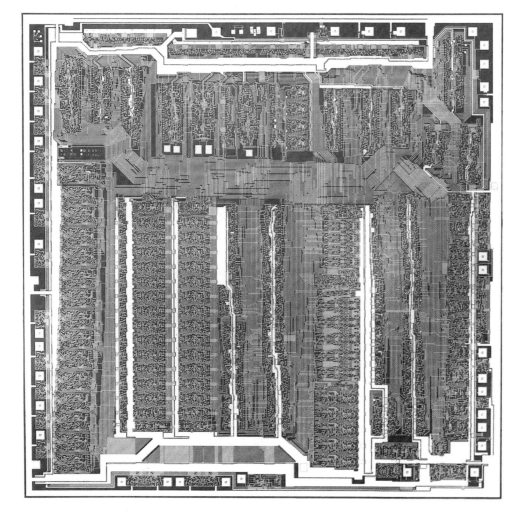

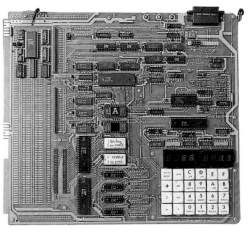

A microprocessor (left), magnified nineteen times to show the individual circuits. Its actual size is seen as the red square below. Such a microprocessor, indicated above as A, is an essential part of the microcomputer (above). This microcomputer, shown with its case removed, is just slightly larger in area than a page of this book.

A robot spray-painting an automobile. Robots easily perform complicated and detailed tasks such as this, and can be reprogrammed to paint different models of car with different colors.

are provided with it then it is a microcomputer. The result is a very small computer, but one with limited facilities. It will not have very much main storage, and it will not be able to handle many input and output devices. But it will be able to calculate almost as fast as a more sophisticated computer, and it is possible to buy a tiny microcomputer that executes instructions as fast as a minicomputer costing hundreds of times the price.

Microprocessors are so small and cheap that they are also used as parts of all kinds of well-known machines. A microprocessor can keep a car cruising at a constant speed, for example. This system, called "cruise control," already exists in many automobiles. The driver reaches a desired speed then tells the microprocessor that he or she wants to keep to that speed by pressing a button. The driver then takes his foot off the accelerator and the microprocessor takes over. It notes the car's speed and if the car starts going slower (it comes to a hill, perhaps) then the microprocessor increases the supply of gas to the engine. If the car starts to accelerate above the designated speed (going downhill, for example) then the microprocessor will decrease the supply of gas.

Microprocessors, or similar chips, are also responsible for all the completely new products that have appeared in recent years, such as video games,

calculators, digital watches, and chess-playing machines.

Industrial robots also use microprocessors. Automatic production lines have been in operation in industry for many years, but industrial robots are now more sophisticated than they have ever been before. There are robots that use an electronic eye to inspect parts coming off a production line, select the ones needed, and then attach them in the correct place to another part. The robot will attach the parts properly even if they are backward or upside-down when it picks them up; it will also reject any unfamiliar parts. Other robots "learn" skilled jobs such as welding cars. An experienced human employee weld's a particular car using equipment which is attached to the robot. The robot will "memorize" the moves that the person makes, and it will itself then be able to repeat those motions in welding other cars. A robot can work more quickly than a human welder and in conditions that humans could not tolerate.

Within a few years, microprocessors will be as common as electric motors are today and almost every machine will include them – there is one in many programmable washing machines, for instance. And these microprocessors will be taken so much for granted that people will hardly notice them.

Several Programs at Once

The different devices that make up modern computers complete their tasks at different speeds, so that some parts have nothing to do while others are working. To overcome this computers can now run several programs at once, a process called multiprogramming.

Imagine that four people are working in an office that produces bills for its customers. Person A collects a card to give to B. The card tells B what items a customer has bought. B asks C the price of each item and then works out the total cost. Finally B hands the card to D, who types out the bill.

Not only is this inefficient, but A, C, and D are a lot slower than B, who is therefore idle for long periods.

This is exactly the situation a computer is in. Person A is the card reader, B is the processor, C is the disk drive, and D is the line printer. The office and the program are doing a typical billing operation. While the program is faster than the human billing office, in both cases all three processes of reading, printing and disk drive are slower than the processing. Although the processor can do an addition in 0.000001 seconds, it has to wait for the preceding operations to be completed, and these have effectively slowed down the processor to less than ten additions per second.

In the early days of computers this did not matter very much, as computers did not have to receive much input or produce much output. But nowadays there are lots of programs to be done in the same computer. There may be thousands of cards but only a few additions for each card. The result is that the processor spends most of its time waiting for the data that it has to work on.

The answer to this problem of time-wasting is multiprogramming. On a large modern computer there will normally be a number of programs, as well as the operating system, in main storage at any one time. Some programs will be doing input or output.

	Device	Task	Time
A	Card reader	Read one card	0.1 second
B	Processor	Do one addition	0.000001 second
C	Disk drive	Read one record	0.025 second
D	Line printer	Print one line	0.06 second

The processor B works much faster than the other equipment. If all the equipment were slowed down so the processor worked at human speeds the card reader would take about 27 hours to read a card.

Others may be waiting for the processor or a device that another program is using, while one program is using the processor.

Because computers work so quickly, the processor seems to be executing all the programs at once. But in fact the processor is only working on one program at a time, doing a little of one and then a little of another. This is called multiprogramming.

There is one problem with multiprogramming. It is easy for programs to take turns with the processor, and there is no problem sharing a disk drive: one program reads data from one place on it, the next program reads data from another place. But what about printing their outputs? A few lines from one program cannot be followed by a few lines from another, as the printed output would be hopelessly confusing.

The answer to this is a technique called spooling. Instead of the lines being printed directly, the data to be printed is stored on disks. After the operating system has finished the individual program, a separate program, the spool program, takes everything that is to be printed and transfers it from the disks to the printer. The spool program is the only one that uses the printer and it prints all the data for one program together, so there is no confusion. It does the same thing for card readers and all the other devices that cannot be shared.

With all these programs, main storage in a large computer system is a very complicated place. There will be several ordinary programs being worked on; the spool program handling the devices that cannot be shared; and the operating system supervising it all.

In a large computer, the programs take turns at using the devices, such as the processor and the disk drive, that can be shared at different times. A spool program stores the data from programs that need to use a device that cannot be shared, such as the printer. This program takes sections of data as the processor finishes them, stores each section in turn on disk until the entire program is complete, and then sends the program to the printer.

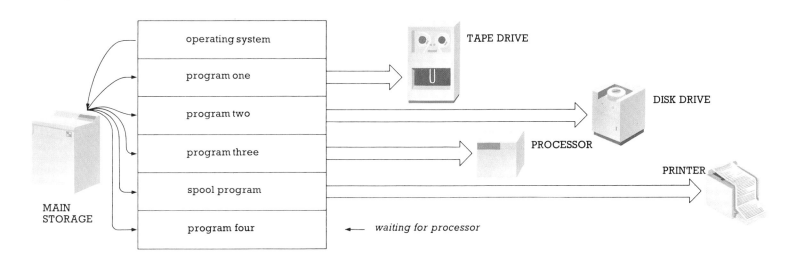

MAIN STORAGE

| operating system |
| program one |
| program two |
| program three |
| spool program |
| program four |

TAPE DRIVE

DISK DRIVE

PROCESSOR

PRINTER

← *waiting for processor*

An overall view of some of the computer equipment used for the space shuttle orbiter aeroflight simulator (OAS) at Johnson Space Center, Houston, on which several programs must be run at once. OAS supports the training of the shuttle's crew and flight controllers by simulating space conditions.

Virtual Storage

On a simple computer every part of every program that is running at any given moment has to be in main storage. This limits the number and size of programs that can be run at any one time. A program only slightly too large for the main storage available would not be able to run at all. It is possible for a programmer to rearrange one large program into many small ones that can run one at a time, but this takes a lot of time and effort. A sophisticated computer overcomes this problem by using the concept of virtual storage. Virtual storage allows the programmer to write his program as though he had much more main storage than actually exists.

Virtual storage is not a physical object such as main storage; it is a concept. The programmer writes a program as though virtual storage did exist but in fact the program will be stored on magnetic disks. Then the operating system divides into parts each of the individual programs it is supervising, puts all those parts onto magnetic disks, and reads into main storage only the parts of the programs needed.

Most programs can be divided into four parts:
1. Initialization: the first instructions in a program that prepare for the rest of the program.
2. Processing normal data: the part of the program that handles normal data. This part is small because it repeats the same few instructions again and again in a loop.
3. Processing abnormal data: the instructions in the program for handling abnormal data – maybe there are errors the program must correct.
4. Termination: the instructions that tidy up at the end of the program.

Suppose a program were 4000 instructions long. There might be 1000 instructions for initialization, 500 for processing normal data, 1500 for processing abnormal data, and 1000 for termination.

If the program runs for a total of one hundred minutes, it might spend ninety of those minutes performing the 500 instructions for handling normal data and only ten minutes performing the other 3500 instructions. However, on a simple computer all 4000 instructions will have to be in main storage for all hundred minutes. So for ninety minutes this program will waste all the main storage that is needed for 3500 instructions, time in which the computer could use this main storage to work on a different program.

Usually the operating system does not know which

A comparative diagram to show what the different parts of a program, represented by zeros and ones, in main storage might look like. Initialization, which starts off the program, processing normal data, and termination, the final stage of the program, are all in main storage for a much longer period than processing abnormal data. However, all 1500 instructions for processing abnormal data must be in main storage for the full 100 minutes of the program because some of the instructions could be needed at any time.

These two programmers are each entering a program at a VDU. Virtual storage enables each of them to write a program that is much bigger than the main storage capacity of the computer they will use.

instructions in a program are concerned with initialization, and which instructions process normal data. So it cannot divide the program into parts that correspond to these functions. To avoid this it can divide the program into small parts of equal size, often called pages. Whenever the processor comes to execute a instruction that is in a page that is not in main storage that page is copied from disk into main storage (the original remains on disk). If there is not enough room in main storage the new page replaces a page that has not been used for a long time. In this way the pages that are being used tend to be in main storage while the pages that are not being used are left on disk.

On a computer with virtual storage the operating system starts the program by trying to perform the first instruction. If this is in a page that is not in main storage the operating system copies that page into main storage before the instruction is performed. As the program goes through initialization it performs all the 1000 associated instructions. As a result the pages containing these instructions are copied

into main storage. After this there is no need to copy any more pages until initialization is complete. Then the program branches to the 500 instructions for handling normal data. It may be that some of these instructions for handling normal data share a page with the instructions for initialization, so they are already in main storage. But most of them are probably on other pages on disks and it is necessary to copy these pages into main storage. These pages replace some of the pages that were used during initialization as many of the initialization pages have not been used for some time. This process continues with the operating system only keeping in main storage the pages that are needed to handle the present task, until finally only the pages needed for termination remain in main storage. As a result the most main storage capacity the program needs is enough to hold the maximum number of pages that are needed at one time, in this case the pages with the 1500 instructions for abnormal data. Without virtual storage the program would need main storage for 4000 instructions.

Timesharing

When many programmers are executing programs simultaneously on the same computer, the process is known as timesharing, because the computer is sharing its time among the programs.

Timesharing is a form of multiprogramming, since the computer is running a number of programs at the same time. Timesharing, however, goes further than multiprogramming since it allows the programmers to communicate with their programs while those programs are being executed. Each programmer writes his program, keys it into his terminal, tells the computer to translate it and then starts it running. He has the impression that he is operating an individual computer on his own and knows nothing of all the other programs being run. The processor attends to each individual program in turn. However, the operating system switches the processor from one program to another so quickly that each program can talk via the terminal to each programmer.

The one great advantage of timesharing is the speed with which the programmer can see the results of his program. Each programmer should have to wait only a few seconds for a response to a request. This means that every program has to be in the processor very frequently to respond speedily to the programmers. Because of this, timesharing is not appropriate for the programs that need to use the processor for a long time. But for short programs – those being tested or changed, for example – it is ideal. One particularly good example of a time-sharing program is one that allows many different individuals working at more or less the same time to request different items of data from a large quantity of scientific information.

Because there may be a great many small programs running at the same time, not all of them can be fitted into main storage together. As a result, the operating system shifts the programs to magnetic disks until they are needed, and then transfers them into main storage. Each programmer is given the illusion that he has all to himself a vast main storage as well as a processor, and does not know that the programs may be on disks. As many as a hundred

A programmer enters his program at a terminal, and the computer responds so quickly that the programmer can operate as though his is the only program on the computer, although there may be many others.

programmers may be able to use the same computer simultaneously.

The alternative to timesharing is for programmers to put their programs on tapes or disks and to give the programs to the computer operator, who runs each program in turn. The operating system makes sure that the correct data is used and prints a report on any errors that arise. This makes efficient use of the computer's time because the computer never has to wait for human intervention. But this system can waste the programmer's time. The programmers might have to wait perhaps several hours for a program to go through the computer before any errors would be detected. Timesharing solves this problem of time-wasting. Programmers can watch the program being processed, correct it if something goes wrong, and start it working again immediately.

program one: a doctor runs a program that analyzes the prevalence of allergies among adult men

program two: a programmer writes a program that calculates how much food the hospital needs in a day

```
= RR-B/(2.
R2 = RR*2−4.0
WRITE (SQRT (AE
GOTO 10 T, 0.0) G(
WR   14, 1  + R
  ST  R1, OUTP
  L   R2, NEX
     4
```

program three: a systems programmer tests for accuracy a newly written program that records the amount of different blood groups stored in the blood bank

The computer in a hospital is used by many different programmers, who may all be in different parts of the building and unaware of the others. A doctor makes calculations on his terminal; an administrator checks the levels of food stocks; while a systems programmer tries out a new program to ensure that the program contains no errors. If any program contains a mistake the person using it can stop the program and check it step by step until he or she finds where the error is.

How Computers Make Mistakes

Almost everyone knows an example of a computer's mistake, such as an electricity bill for zero dollars and zero cents which continues to be sent until the company receives a check for that amount. Cases like this are a nuisance and they are often thought of as a joke. However, there have been much more serious errors. The United States has gone onto false nuclear alert at least three times because of computer warnings. Bomber crews had started up the engines of their planes before officials discovered that the computer warnings were in error. This shows just how serious computer mistakes can be.

Computers make mistakes in lots of different ways. The electricity bill for zero dollars and zero cents might have been an error by the programmer who wrote the program that calculated and printed the bills. Perhaps he assumed that everyone would use some electricity and did not allow for someone not

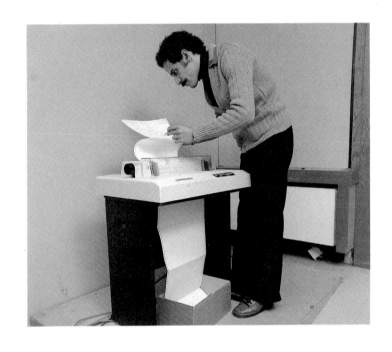

This programmer uses a terminal to submit programs for testing (left), and then inspects the output on a printer (above). Systematically checking and testing programs like this is one way of finding mistakes.

using any who should not be charged anything, or perhaps he miscoded the instruction that the program should not print any bills for zero dollars. Programming errors can be allowed for by checking the results, perhaps with a different program.

The false nuclear alerts were probably not programming errors. The details are a secret, but apparently one alert was caused by someone entering on the computer a tape that contained test data. This tape of data was used to test the computer system and it gave the computer the impression that the United States was being attacked. If that was the cause of the alert, then it is an example of the other classic computer mistake: the introduction of either wrong or faulty data. There is a saying in the computer business: garbage in, garbage out. This means that bad data will produce bad results.

For this reason as much effort needs to be put into collecting good data as into processing it. A lot of the data that is keyed onto magnetic tape, disks or punched cards is keyed in twice, once to enter the data in the first place and then a second time, by someone else, to check it. There are machines that can compare what the first and second operators have entered and warn of any differences between the two before the data ever reaches the computer.

Nevertheless, some bad data often seems to get through to the computer. Most computer systems therefore have a program to check the data before the real processing begins. For example, a program to store details of automobile license numbers would need data about the numbers, the automobiles and the drivers' names and addresses. Before the program is run that actually stores the information, another program would probably be run to ensure the data was reasonable. This program would check that the license numbers were valid, that no number was duplicated, and that all the makes of car were real.

Another way of checking a program for errors is to put the data on punched cards. After this has been done in a punched-card machine, the cards are put in a machine called a card verifier and the same information is typed on the keyboard. The verifier does not punch holes, but checks that the holes were punched correctly the first time.

Neither programming errors nor data errors are the results of the hardware going wrong. Computer hardware does go wrong, but when it does the effects are usually noticeable very quickly – the processor will stop working, or the printer will release a continuous stream of blank pages.

People are trying to find ways of designing computers and programming languages so that programmers are less likely to make mistakes. It is vital to find ways of writing programs that have fewer errors in them and to find ways of cutting out bad data. This may be one of the most important areas of research in the next few years.

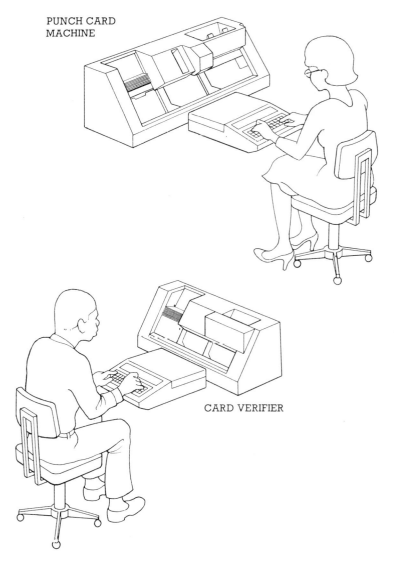

PUNCH CARD MACHINE

CARD VERIFIER

Computers Fix Their Own Faults

Any complicated machine is potentially full of small errors. Large computer systems are no exception; they may make small errors at any time. Although electronic chips are very reliable, there are so many transistors and other components on them that the chances are quite high of one going wrong somewhere. Also, many devices, such as printers and tape drives, have mechanical parts that are likely to break down.

As in all machines, faults and errors must be detected and corrected. While a bit changing accidentally from a one to a zero may seem a minor detail in a large program, such a small error can have serious consequences. Suppose that bit were part of a number that represented a salary. You would certainly think it important if you were suddenly paid $0000 instead of $1000. With computers, any small error can be important, and it is difficult to anticipate which errors will matter and which will not.

Because of this, a computer has to check itself all the time. It must at least know something has gone wrong so that it does not print out the wrong results. There are many ways of doing this, but one of the most common methods uses something called a parity bit. Data recorded on magnetic tape is recorded on six or eight tracks, and there is a seventh or ninth track that is not actually used for data. This track contains the parity bit. This is either a zero or a one so that the total number of ones on all tracks is even. This is even parity; in odd parity the number of ones on the tracks is odd. Whether the parity is even or odd depends on the manufacturer.

As it reads the data, the computer checks that the parity always stays even or odd. If it changes, then the computer knows something has gone wrong and it will signal the fault, possibly by stopping the program and displaying a message.

Parity bits or a similar check are used throughout the computer system, not just on magnetic tape. They are also used on silicon chips, for example. Data may be checked whenever it is read from main storage, or passes to or from another device.

Since we depend so heavily on computer systems, it is becoming more and more important to make them reliable. Often a modern computer does not just detect that a bit is incorrect. It actually locates the bit in error and corrects it so that the program is not interrupted. It can do this because there are many extra bits that are used for this and not to store data. A parity bit is an example of this, but many more extra bits are needed when it is necessary to actually locate and correct the error. Sometimes a large computer has a small service processor attached which does nothing but check the large main processor.

It is all very well to make the computer hardware reliable, but nearly all large computer programs contain mistakes, as they have been programmed by a human being who is liable to error. The software often causes more system failures than all the hardware put together. Some operating systems can help to correct mistakes in the programs. Others just make sure that once a mistake is discovered the programmer has the information to correct it quickly.

Data Bits	Parity Bits	Total
01010011	1	5
00000000	1	1
11100000	0	3
10101101	1	6
00000000	1	1
11110000	1	5
01101111	1	7
10001100	0	3
01110000	0	3
11101000	1	5

One way to check for errors in a program is to use parity bits. The bit on the parity track must always be such that the total number of ones is an odd number. If a bit in any track changes so that the total number becomes even, as it has in the fourth line, the parity bit shows that one of the data bits is wrong.

It is possible for experts to rectify software mistakes by connecting a terminal in their own office to the computer, which may be many miles away, and then inspecting the problem by using the terminal. Nevertheless, making software reliable is one of the biggest problems facing the computer industry.

The operator here is using a special-purpose computer to test the electric circuits seen through the screen at top. Although some circuits can automatically correct their own errors they cannot do this unless they are mechanically right.

Computers that Speak, Listen, and Draw

You may have seen films set in the future in which people talk directly to a computer and the computer replies in an almost human voice. Is that possible, or is it just a wild flight of the imagination?

There are already computers that can speak. Some modern automobiles have small computers that detect certain conditions, such as the gas running low or the seat belt being undone. The computer uses spoken output to warn the driver about the condition. There is even one computer that is designed to read ordinary printed books to the blind. It is not perfect and it sometimes gets a word wrong, but the listener can usually work out from the context what the word should be.

The display (above) shows a graph of the speech pattern of the sentence "where are you?" Computers respond to the spoken word by converting sounds to patterns of bits. The computer then studies the patterns to determine which words they represent and draws a graph of the patterns.

The industrial designer at left is using a light pen to draw the circuits of a silicon chip on a VDU screen.

Computers can take sound as input too. In digital recording, for instance, a computer takes music as input and converts it into bits. The bits are then used to produce the music on records and tapes without any loss of accuracy. But understanding sound in the form of speech presents an extra problem. The same word can be pronounced in a totally different way by different people, or even by the same person at different times.

Nevertheless, there has been some progress. There are computer-controlled wheelchairs that obey spoken commands such as "right," "left," and "stop." But there are very few computers that can accept sentences as opposed to a single word of input. And those computers that accept a single word often have a particularly limited vocabulary. Only a few selected words can be used, and they have to be carefully pronounced.

Some computers can be programmed to recognize particular words. Examples of the words they have to recognize, spoken by the people who will be speaking them, are given to computers. In this way the machines can pick out different pronunciations of the same word by different people.

It is likely that computers will get better at recognizing spoken words in the next few years. Recognizing a sound as being a particular word is somewhat like recognizing a mark on a piece of paper as being a particular number or letter. They are both examples of the problem that computer scientists call pattern recognition. Computers have been able to read good handwritten numbers for a long time. It is more difficult for them to recognize speech, but the same principles are involved.

So far, input and output have been seen as letters, numbers, or words, but computers can also accept and display pictures. There is a kind of terminal, similar to a VDU, called a graphics screen, which is very popular among designers of everything from airplanes, cars and houses to computers and silicon chips. The computer program displays on the screen a picture of the object that is being designed, and it is possible for an operator to change the design by pointing at the screen with an instrument called a light pen. When the light pen is pressed against the screen a signal is sent to the computer indicating where on the screen it was pressed. If the designer wants to add a line joining two points together he

This small personal computer can be used for a variety of tasks. Here, it has been programmed to draw pictures on the screen of an ordinary television. This is useful for anyone dealing with visual media.

presses the light pen against one point then moves it to the other; the computer is programmed to display a new line connecting those two points. The computer will note the changes and can then work out the consequences – how a change will affect the space for passengers in a car, for example. The computer can also rotate the design to show what the changes will look like from different angles.

Graphics screens are also used in designing new roads. The size of the road and the route it will take are described to the computer. The computer can then present on the graphics screen a moving picture that shows what the road will look like to a motorist driving along it. In this way problems – such as places where the driver has a bad view of the right of way – can be found before the road is built. To present a moving picture on a graphics screen means that the computer has to make a lot of calculations very quickly. As computers are getting faster and faster this type of application may be one of the major uses of computers in the future.

Unusual Storage Devices

The processor can receive data about 100,000 times more quickly from main storage than it can from disk. Computer users, however, often want a way of storing data that is cheaper than main storage and faster than disks.

One possible alternative type of storage is on magnetic bubble chips. Magnetic bubbles depend on an odd effect that happens when certain substances on chips are magnetized. Most of the substance is magnetized, but within it there will also be microscopic "bubbles." These bubbles are about a 25,000th of an inch across, and there may be tens of thousands of them on a chip. They are not really bubbles, as they contain no air; they are just small parts of the substance which have been magnetized in a different way from the rest of the substance. Each bubble, or the absence of one, is used to represent a bit of information. By rapidly varying a magnetic field that surrounds each chip, the bubbles move around the chip at great speed and there is just one place on the chip where they are detected. To read the bit that a bubble represents involves waiting until

the bubble comes to that place. This is slower than reading the bits in main storage but far faster than using disks and tapes.

Bubble storage will never be as fast as main storage because there will be a delay while the bubble comes to the place where it can be detected. However, it has one important advantage: if the power is switched off the bubbles remain, so the data stored is not lost.

Something is also needed to fill the gap between disks and tapes. Some computer installations have tens of thousands of tapes full of data that may be needed at some time or another. Magnetic tape is very cheap, but the time required to find the correct

One of the latest types of magnetic bubble devices magnified 220 times. The V-shaped marks are tiny pieces of metal which direct the bubbles. The bubbles themselves cannot be seen with the naked eye.

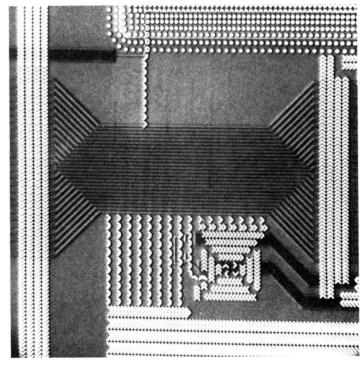

On circuits using magnetic bubble chips there is one place where bubbles are created, and another where they are read, so the time it takes before a bubble can be read will depend on how far around the loop it has to go.

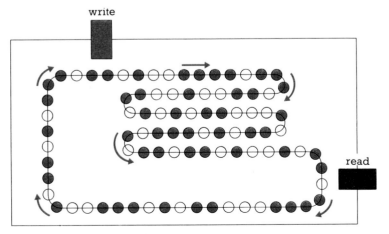

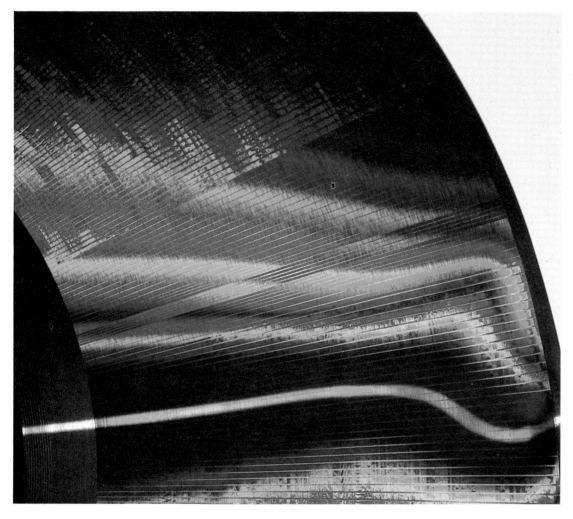

A photograph of a section of an optical disk. Many more bits per inch can be put onto an optical disk than onto a magnetic disk because the laser beam that reads the bits can detect them even when they are very close together.

tape and mount it is very high by computer standards. The answer to this speed problem may be mass storage devices, which are like automatic tape libraries. The information is kept in cartridges similar to magnetic tape, but operators do not need to find the appropriate cartridge and mount it, as the mass storage device itself automatically locates it and mounts it on a special reader when told to do so by the computer. The result is that vast quantities of data can be made available within a few seconds. One mass storage device can hold 250,000 million characters, enough to store fifty characters of information about every person in the entire world. Any item of data can be reached in a few seconds and the whole device fits into a medium-sized room.

These are two of the most important examples of new ways of storing data. Optical disks are another development. These disks have holes burned into their reflective surface which are detected by a laser beam. The presence of a hole represents a one bit and the absence of a hole represents a zero bit, or vice versa. A device such as this can be fast, but the data, once written, cannot be changed. Other new storage devices are being developed and every year new possibilities are discovered, while at the same time the old favorites, such as magnetic disks, get faster.

Supercool Computers

The most powerful computers of the 1990s will be up to a hundred times faster than the present ones. They will fit into a cube a few inches in size, and they will have to be kept at about −440°F.

These future computers are based on two extraordinary phenomena that physicists have known about for many years: superconductivity and tunneling.

At room temperature all substances, even the best conductors, resist electricity to some extent. This means it is necessary to keep applying a voltage in order to make electricity flow through the substance, and some heat is generated by the electricity flowing. However, at temperatures very close to absolute zero (−459.69°F), some substances have no resistance to electricity at all. The current, once started, will keep flowing forever without any more voltage being applied and, most importantly, without generating any heat. A substance that behaves in this way is called a superconductor.

The other phenomenon is tunneling. This occurs when two conductors (not necessarily superconductors) are held very close together with an insulator between them. Normally an insulator will stop any electricity from flowing through. But if the insulating barrier is thin enough the electricity appears to tunnel through it and a small current flows between the two conductors. For this to happen the insulator must be less than half a millionth of an inch thick.

The same effect is achieved when superconductors are used. However, in their case no electricity will flow if the insulator is then magnetized, for the insulator will become very resistant to the electric current. Because of this, the one bit can be represented by the flow of current and the zero bit by the lack of electricity (or vice versa) that occurs when the insulator is magnetized.

A circuit such as this is called a Josephson junction after the British physicist Brian Josephson, who predicted the effect in the late 1960s. Josephson junctions are still at an experimental stage, but they may replace silicon chips as the basis of the computers of the future. They contain all that is necessary for computer memory: a circuit that is in one of two electric states to represent the bits.

Such circuits will work much faster than ordinary silicon chip transistors because they can be switched from a positive to a negative state even more quickly. And since they generate no heat – unlike conventional circuits that would melt if packed closer together than they are now – these circuits can be built in very much smaller units than are possible at present. This is important because the speed of

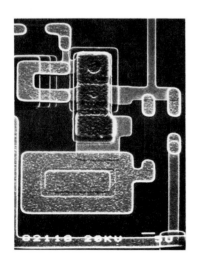
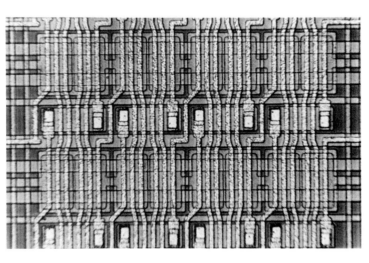

At left is a segment of an experimental storage chip that uses Josephson junctions. There are sixteen circuits (one of them, magnified four thousand times, is on the far left), each capable of holding a bit. These circuits can switch on or off in thirteen trillionths of a second – ten times faster than the fastest transistor in an ordinary computer.

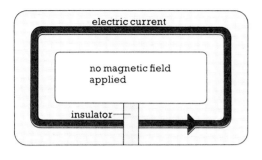

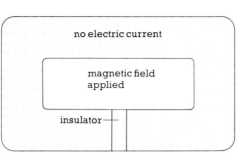

A loop of superconductor has a thin insulator breaking the loop. If there is no magnetic field (far left), a current will flow forever — this could represent a one bit. When a magnetic field is applied (left), the insulator resists electricity and the current stops. This could represent a zero bit.

computers at the moment is limited by the time it takes electricity to travel from one part of the computer to another. If the units are smaller, the electricity will not have so far to travel and the computer can operate more quickly.

But there will be difficulties in building Josephson junction computers. Since they have to be kept at about −440°F they must be placed in a refrigerator. The refrigerator is not a problem, as there have been adequate refrigerators at temperatures of about absolute zero for many years. But the computer will be very inaccessible and any breakdowns will be expensive to repair because to do so would involve heating the computer to room temperature very slowly so as not to destroy the Josephson junctions. As a result the computer would be out of action for a long time, which most companies would find impractical.

The greatest problem with Josephson junctions, however, is making the insulator between the two superconductors thin enough. Apart from its thinness, it also must be accurate to the diameter of a few atoms. Despite these problems, computer circuits incorporating Josephson junctions have been made and are being used experimentally in the United States and Europe.

A computer research scientist lowers a circuit chip composed of nearly 4500 Josephson junctions into a container of liquid helium, whose temperature is only a few degrees above absolute zero.

Supercomputers

Some computer applications, such as weather forecasting and air traffic control, use all the speed that any computer can currently provide and still need more. This has led to the development of supercomputers that may already be hundreds or even thousands of times faster than an ordinary computer. How do they work so fast?

Supercomputers achieve their speeds by working on more than one instruction at once. One way of doing this is by having a sort of assembly line, with each instruction at a different stage of the line. While the processor brings the instruction from main storage, it is working out the address for some data, bringing a different item of data from main storage, following the instruction for another item, and storing the result of yet another. By doing this, several instructions are overlapped. In contrast to this method, a normal computer will complete each

The CRAY I supercomputer, at the top right of the photograph, can make over 100 million multiplications a second. In the foreground is a conventional computer that supplies the CRAY I with data.

instruction before it begins the next one, which obviously reduces the speed at which it can process data.

It is all very well working on one instruction before the computer has finished the previous one, but if the previous instruction had been a branch the computer might never execute the following instruction at all, as it would follow the branch. Because of this, the assembly line technique can only work well if there are not too many branches.

An alternative to the assembly line technique is for the computer to take a single instruction and apply it to lots of items of data at once. Suppose a large group of numbers all need to be multiplied by twenty. A conventional computer would take each number from main storage to the processor, one at a time, multiply it by twenty, and then put the result back. Some supercomputers can put all the numbers in a special memory and then send the memory the instruction "multiply by twenty." Every number in the memory would be multiplied by twenty simultaneously. The larger the special memory, the more numbers can be processed at once and therefore the

This schematic diagram shows a supercomputer that uses an assembly line for working on several instructions at once. Instruction 1 has been completed, and instructions 2, 3, 4 and 5 are being processed. When instruction 2 is complete, instruction 6 will go to the processor.

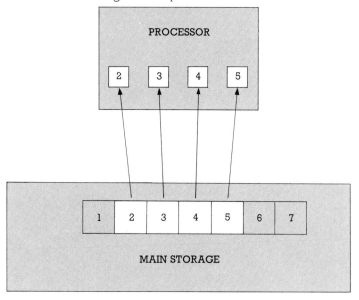

faster the computer can work. So a computer like this can go very fast provided there are large amounts of data that are to be treated in the same way. Some applications are obviously not suitable for this, for example a long calculation in which each stage depends on the results of the previous one.

Another way in which supercomputers achieve their high speeds is by special methods of searching for data. Normally an item of data in storage is referred to by the address of its location. This means that if someone wants to find a particular item, for example a teacher wanting to find out which student achieved the highest marks in a math examination, the computer searches through the addresses for each student until it can give the correct answer. Some supercomputers, however, have memories in which every address is searched simultaneously; the memory then returns the appropriate data immediately.

Supercomputers take advantage of the many ways for increasing a computer's speed. Speed can depend on how the computer is organized – whether it can perform many instructions simultaneously, for example – and the nature of the work that it is doing. The organization of a computer is known as its architecture. The architecture of most computers is very similar at the moment, but a great deal of research is being done which may show that it is just as important as new types of chip or new storage devices.

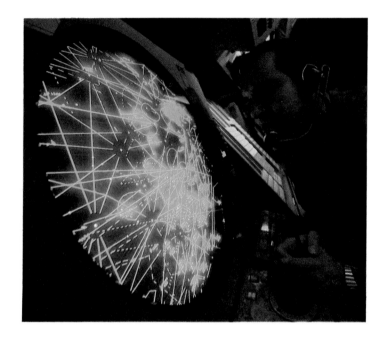

This air traffic control display screen is one of many linked to a supercomputer at air traffic control on Long Island, New York. Each monitoring device like this is assigned to a fixed area of airspace. The operator in charge of this screen must follow the progress of each plane flying into and out of the area.

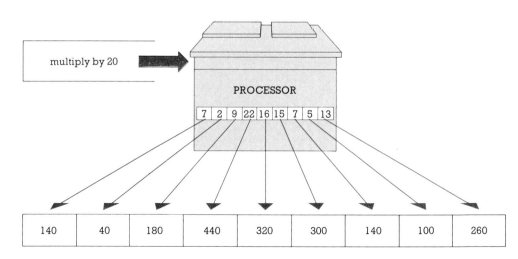

This stylized diagram shows a supercomputer executing one instruction – multiply by twenty – on several numbers simultaneously. Some computers can do the same operation on several hundred numbers at once.

Computers and the Telephone

Terminals and other input and output devices need to be connected to the processor in some way, not necessarily by special cable. Anything that will transmit a telephone call, such as an ordinary telephone wire or the satellites used for international telephone calls, will also transmit computer data. Any device that can be connected to the processor directly can also be connected to it over a distance of thousands of miles by the telephone network. That is how an airline reservations clerk can use a terminal in New York to talk to a computer in London.

There are even some portable terminals that can be carried around and then connected to the computer wherever there is a convenient telephone (a pay phone can be used if the caller has enough coins). This can be very useful, for example, for an engineer who wants to use the computer but is always traveling. He or she would have to know the computer's telephone number. Then it is a simple matter of putting the receiver into a special converter called an acoustic coupler attached to the portable terminal. The coupler, in turn, acts as interpreter between the terminal and the distant computer. Using the same equipment, the engineer can even work at home and use his or her own telephone. A computer system like this has to have a password – either a word or a number – for all its users, otherwise anyone who had an acoustic coupler could dial the computer's number and start using the machine.

Computers take up a very small portion of the telephone network at the moment, but that portion is growing very fast. There may be a time when there is more phone conversation between computers than there is between people. In fact, there is a real danger that the telephone network will not be able to handle all this computer work. Local telephone calls are normally sent as electric signals along the wires and cables that we know as telephone lines. If, in the future, we had to rely on these for all computer communication then we could soon run out of capacity. But there are alternatives.

Besides traveling along cables, telephone calls are transmitted in much the same way as television pictures, using microwaves. Microwaves can travel only in straight lines, so each transmitter has to be on a line of sight above the earth's horizon with the receiver. That is why microwave transmitters are always on high towers. Unfortunately, a chain of them cannot be built across the oceans. It was because of this that the telephone companies turned to communication satellites in the late 1950s. Three well-

This telephone receiver has been inserted into an acoustic coupler, which links the terminal in the photograph to a computer. The coupler converts the data that is keyed into the terminal into impulses that are sent along the telephone wire to the computer. The coupler then converts the response from the computer into the words and numbers the terminal displays on the screen.

placed satellites can cover almost the whole world.

Satellites have made a vast contribution to telephone capacity, and therefore to computer communications, but there may be problems relating to satellites in the future. There is one orbit, called the geosynchronous orbit, that is clearly the best place to put a satellite, because once placed in such an orbit the satellite stays in the same position relative to the earth. But satellites cannot be placed too close together or they interfere with each other. The result is that this particular orbit is getting full. In fact, all the positions over North and South America have been taken. Spacing requirements are currently under review to see if it is possible to place satellites closer together.

A new method of transmitting telephone calls – and thus computer data – is by using optical fibers. This method uses light instead of electricity to send the signals. It works by sending the signal on a light beam that is directed along a glass tube about as thin as a human hair. These tubes can be run underground with a protective covering. A light beam can carry so many signals at once that optical fibers should allow us to send all the messages we could possibly want in the foreseeable future. Optical fibers are already being used in England and the United States, though it will be many decades before they are common.

The telephone system is a great help to computers, but it works the other way around as well. Until recently a telephone was a telephone and that was about it. But now we have "intelligent" telephones and telephone exchanges that use computers. A computerized telephone exchange can transform an office. If you make a call and the line of the person you are calling is busy, you can dial another digit which will instruct the computer to call you both back when the other person has finished. Incoming calls to your own number can be redirected automatically to another number and the caller need not know that he is speaking to you on a different number from the one he dialed. Any number of calls can be combined so each caller can hear all the others in one teleconference. If many calls are made which use a long number – such as overseas calls – then an abbreviated form can be dialed on the telephone which tells the computer itself to dial the full number. The possibilities are almost endless.

Communications satellites, such as this one, are the cheapest way of transmitting large quantities of computer data over very long distances.

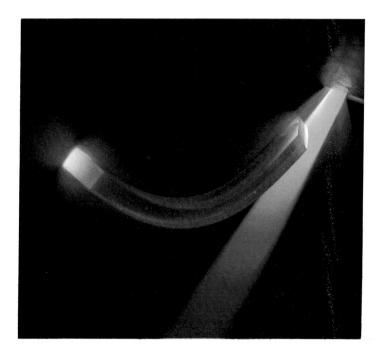

Light normally travels in a straight line, but in optical fibers, such as this one, light will follow the threads of the fibers even if the threads are curved.

73

Connecting Computers Together

Computers have been connected to each other almost from the moment they were invented. Apart from systems being linked over thousands of miles, many processors can be tied into main storage in the same room. Nowadays a machine that appears to be one fast processor to the user is often a number of microprocessors working together.

Early computers were divided into simple machines that were good at input and output (for commercial use) and more sophisticated machines that were good at scientific calculation. A popular combination was to use one of the cheaper commercial machines to prepare the data for the scientific machine. The first machine would read in the cards or tape and then pass the data across to the other machine. The scientific machine would make the calculations and then pass the results back, and the commercial machine would print the results. In that way they were both doing what they were good at.

The same situation is still found in very large installations, but on a much larger scale. For example, some users, such as aerospace companies and major banks, need so much computer power that they have five or six of the very largest commercial processors all connected together. One of the processors is the master that looks after all the input and output. As work arrives the master sends it to one of the other processors and divides up the work so that all the other processors are kept busy. Each processor will finish a program every few minutes. Technicians must make sure that all the processors are kept supplied with the correct programs, and that two processors are not given programs that conflict by needing the same magnetic disk or tape at the same time.

Other organizations use more than one complete computer system because they must have a spare one. For example, many railroad companies have a computer to record the positions of all the trains that are not in use. Indeed, most modern railroads cannot

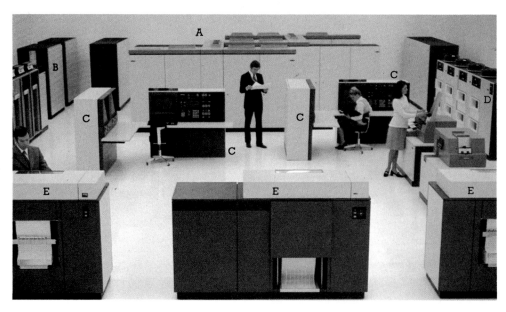

In this computer system the three rows of cabinets (A) at the back of the room contain two processors and main storage – which the processors share. The programs can run on either processor. The other devices in the system are: tape drives (B), operating consoles (C), disk drives (D), and printers (E).

Every aspect of the flight of the space shuttle shown blasting off from the Kennedy Space Center, Florida, is controlled by computers at the site and elsewhere. As soon as the shuttle clears the takeoff tower, Mission Control at Houston (right) takes over. It is the same for each manned space flight. The various display consoles are all linked to computers and monitor conditions on the flight – the health of the crew, the shuttle's trajectory, speed at reentry and the final touchdown.

operate efficiently without a computer since they need to know the exact whereabouts of each train before the trains can be called into use. Because of this, the companies maintain two computers in case one goes wrong. Each computer handles different types of work, and both can read in the record of the trains' locations. Either machine can then be used if the other one fails. In some applications – such as aircraft control and space flights – lives may be at stake if a computer fails.

There are other ways in which computers can be made to cooperate, some currently in use and some still experimental. As in most computer projects, the greatest difficulties and problems are not with the hardware but with the software. For example, if there are two or more programs running on different processors and working on the same data, they may interfere with each other. Suppose that two programs are working on an airline reservations system. One of them might offer the last remaining seat on a flight to a person in Boston while the other offered the same seat to a person in Toronto. To avoid this, one program must wait until the other has finished with the data on that flight before the other program can use that data. But if there are too many items of data like this, then one program spends most of its time waiting and the system will not go much faster than it would with one program on one processor.

This problem of waiting to use an item of data also applies to devices such as printers and terminals, and even to locations in main storage. If it were not for this, it would be possible to make almost any computer system more powerful simply by adding more processors. This problem limits the ways in which computers can be usefully connected – adding just another processor to a computer system very rarely increases the processing power in proportion. Nevertheless, there are tremendous benefits in getting computers to communicate with each other and it is more and more common for an organization to have many connected computers.

Computer Networks

Because computers can be connected together internationally, there can be whole networks of computers around the world. One computer company, for example, keeps a record of any faults on all its equipment throughout the world. There are two copies of this record, one on a computer in the United States, the other on a computer in England. The two computers keep each other up to date about any new faults by communicating with each other. But there can be more than one or two computers cooperating. There may be ten, twenty, or even hundreds of computers around the world, all communicating with one another. Each computer can have its own terminals which may also be spread over thousands of miles. The result is a worldwide network of computers and terminals.

In some networks the computers cooperate so closely that a terminal user may not even know which country it is in. For example, imagine a salesman in England who works for a large multinational company with its headquarters in the United States. He types in his request on a terminal in his office in London and asks for a particular computer service, say some data on the latest sales figures. As far as he is concerned he just types in his request to a computer. Actually, he is activating a multinational system, because his request is transferred to a computer in New York.

The answer might take a few seconds to be displayed at the salesman's terminal if the lines were busy or someone else were using the same program. If the salesman waits for the results of his request he may notice the delay. Certainly it would take minutes or even hours to send a large quantity of data. But this is likely to change with advances in technology.

Computer networks using telephone lines will not be used just for computer data. They can be used for voices, as is an ordinary telephone network, or even for sending pictures and text, such as letters and reports. Science fiction stories often suggest that in the distant future there will be a data network surrounding the whole world. They are wrong only in one respect – the future is almost here.

The Society for Worldwide Interbank Financial Telecommunications (SWIFT), an international association of banks based in Belgium, uses computers to speed up international business transactions. Member banks use a network of computers to transfer money between their branches in North and South America, Europe and the Far East. A message can get from one computer to any other in less than ten seconds.

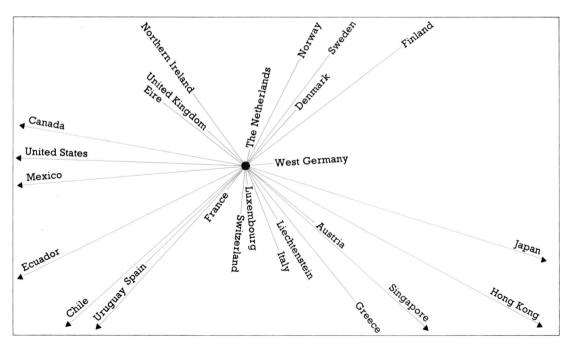

76

Computer communications within a large multi-national corporation can be very complex. A request typed into a terminal in Detroit may go through the following stages:

1. The request goes by telephone to a computer in Detroit that is connected to all the Detroit terminals. It takes messages from the terminals and passes them by telephone to a computer in New York.

2. The New York computer does not have the relevant program. It sends the request to a computer in Paris. This time the telephone link is made by satellite.

3. The computer in Paris knows of two computers that have the data, one in Marseilles and one in London. The circuit to Marseilles is out of order so the computer routes the message by telephone to the one in London.

4. The computer in London deals with the request and sends the reply back to Paris. The reply then returns to Detroit via New York. It must use the same route because otherwise the system would be almost impossible to control.

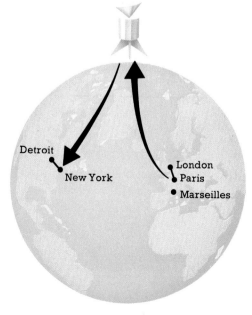

Televisions and Computers

There is little difference in principle between a computer's VDU and an ordinary television set. They both have cathode ray tubes, and the picture they display comes from an electric signal. For a television to be used as a VDU, an output signal from the computer has to be substituted for the normal television signal. A cheap personal computer that can be used at home will very likely be plugged into an ordinary television set.

This is not the only way a TV is used as a terminal. Ordinary TV sets are now used in some countries as terminals to large computer networks. These services are provided by video data systems, such as the two typical systems called teletext and viewdata. In each case, a computer stores a wide range of information which people at home or work can select and display on the television screen.

A TV screen showing some of the subjects on which information can be obtained by the viewdata system. The viewer chooses the subject by tapping its number into the keyboard provided with the TV.

The information available on both teletext and viewdata is generally the same type as that found in newspapers, but because the information is kept on a computer, fresh details can be fed in continuously. As soon as something happens, the new facts can be placed on the computer and anyone using a television as a computer terminal will receive the latest data. A businessman can get the latest stock market prices, and a sports fan can get the latest scores. There are also games, puzzles, recipes, and anything else that might be of interest to the average television viewer.

Data from a teletext computer is broadcast in the same way as ordinary TV programs, although a slightly more sophisticated television set than normal is needed to receive it. This TV displays the data as text or pictures instead of a TV program, or in special cases, superimposed on an ordinary TV picture. It is a oneway process and no message can be sent back to the computer. The teletext computer can transmit all the data it holds to every television screen in the system. But the television cannot display all the data. Instead, the user selects the information he or she requires with a small keyboard. One important potential use of teletext is to provide subtitles to television programs for the deaf and hard of hearing.

Viewdata gives more facilities than teletext. Again a special television is used with a keyboard attached, but now the television is connected to the computer by a telephone line. Instead of leading into an ordinary telephone, the user's telephone line also leads into the viewdata television. This means that you can use viewdata to send data to the computer as well as receive it, and in fact using viewdata is the same as having a conversation with the computer. The user selects the information by pressing numbers on the keyboard which are sent to the computer via the telephone line. The numbers identify a page of information which the computer sends back via the

Viewdata is likely to become an increasingly important means of transmitting data from computer to television. The data is transmitted along a telephone line that is linked to a TV set.

The message travels through the telephone network (indicated by the circle) to the central viewdata computer.

The viewdata computer responds by sending a page of data back to the TV set. The computer can provide over a million pages of information.

In viewdata, the keyboard sends a message along the telephone line. The telephone registers engaged while the viewdata service is being used, though the receiver is in place.

The TV set is also able to receive conventional TV programs.

Terminals supply fresh information to the computer.

A keyboard is used in viewdata to select the pages. The keyboard can either be remote control, similar to the ones that change TV stations, or be connected by wire to the TV set.

telephone line and which is displayed on the television screen.

Companies that want to put information on viewdata design their own pictures – pages of text or diagrams – which the computer then stores. Anyone who has a suitable television can receive the pictures by dialing into the service. Because it is a two-way process the person inspecting the picture can also send information to the computer. You can ask which plays are being performed at which theaters, for

example, and then order tickets through the keyboard of the computer.

Viewdata is still quite expensive and the number of users is therefore small. Besides the special television, you have to pay for the telephone call and a charge is made for the pictures you look at; sometimes the companies supplying the information make a charge too. In spite of the cost, this is a system by which every home could be linked to a computer.

Keeping Data Safe

Information about most people in the advanced western nations is recorded on some computer, somewhere: their medical histories, examination results, criminal records, any money they may have borrowed, the states of their bank accounts, tax records. The list grows every month. With this information computerized people can get at it more easily – if they are allowed to.

That is why so many people are worried about the safety of data on computers. In fact, from the earliest days of computers, experts have been concerned about finding ways to make information secure. Many police forces, for example, keep computer data about known criminals and about people they suspect of crimes. Before computers, they would have kept the files locked in a safe, and anyone who wanted to look at them would have needed permission from whoever had the key. But with a computer system people may want to get the information quickly from a computer that may be miles away. How do we make sure that only authorized personnel have access to the information?

The most popular way is to give a password to those people who are allowed to use the computer. The computer is programmed to ask anyone who uses a terminal to type in the password before that person can do anything else on the computer. A person who does not know the password will not be able to use the computer. An alternative is to give each user a magnetic card. For example, the cash-issuing terminals in banks read a magnetic card and then ask the customer to type in a personal number that must agree with the card. But cards can be lost or stolen, numbers and passwords can be forgotten or copied. If it is very important to keep data secure, then there are even better safeguards that use some personal characteristic of the user. Some terminals have a special pad that the user has to sign, for example. The pad can tell whose signature it is not just by the shape of the letters but by the speed and pressure of the pen. There are other terminals that can recognize people's fingerprints or even their voices.

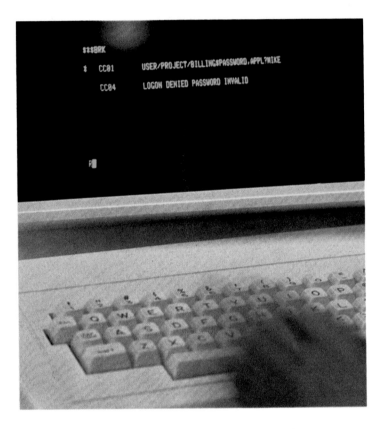

A programmer has typed into the terminal a password that, if correct, would have allowed him to continue and alter the program. In this case the password was wrong and the computer will reject all commands until it receives the correct password. "Logon" is the name of the program that validates the password.

Some computers can do even better than that: magnetic tapes or disks can also be stolen, copied and lost, but the computer can put all the data in a coded form. Even if an unauthorized person did get hold of the data, he or she would not be able to read it. The American National Standards Institute has recommended a code called the Data Encryption Algorithm. It is very likely that most civilian computers throughout the western world will use the code (military computers employ even more sophisticated codes).

Data Encryption Algorithm is a kind of code that uses a number called a key, and no one can decode the message unless he or she knows which key is used. A simple example of a code that uses a key is one in which all the letters in the message are replaced by letters that are a fixed number of places farther on in the alphabet. The key is the number of places farther on that was used when coding the message. For example, if the key were two then A would be replaced by C, B by D, and so on (Y would be replaced by A and Z by B). This code would be very easy to break even if the key were not known, but it would be very difficult to break the Data Encryption Algorithm without the key. Of course, it is possible to try all the keys in turn until the right one is found. The simple code in the example allows for only twenty-six possible keys. The Data Encryption Algorithm, however, allows for so many that a sophisticated computer sysytem working flat out day and night would take about ninety years to find the right key.

At present, very little data is coded using the Data Encryption Algorithm, but soon governments may make it illegal for manufacturers and users not to use the Algorithm for certain types of data. Already laws are being proposed which require all computer manufacturers to develop ways of keeping data safe.

Many organizations employ stringent security systems that permit only certain people into the computer room. In one system, each person has a coded card that must be inserted into a machine, shown at the turnstile (right), and a personal number entered onto the keyboard before the steel turnstile will open. More complex systems recognize not cards and numbers but fingerprints and palmprints (below).

The End of Cash?

Computers are about to make an enormous change in the way we use money. It may take a long time, but the process of making cash obsolete has already started.

Of course, we already make purchases without using cash. We use checks or credit cards, both of which depend heavily on computers to keep a record of how much money is being added and debited. But checks and credit cards are only a different method of decreasing one computerized bank account and increasing another. The process takes a long time and signatures can be forged.

A person who wants to use cash to buy something will either cash a check or use a card to get the money from a cash-issuing terminal at a bank or even in a department store. But does cash have to change hands at all? The cash serves no important function in the transaction, because for goods to change hands

only a few computer records have to be amended. This could be done by one computer talking to the other, or by the store's computer talking to both the computer at its own bank and the one at the shopper's bank.

There could soon be a system in which each person has a special card, with a special number which only the cardholder knows encoded on it magnetically. Whenever a purchase is made, the card is entered into a terminal at the store. The salesperson keys in the amount and the card itself, and asks the shopper for his or her personal number which is also keyed in. The terminal asks the computer to check the shopper's bank account to make sure there is enough credit. If there is, the computer signals its acceptance and automatically decreases the shopper's account and increases the store's. Such cashless ways of shopping are already starting to happen,

This diagram shows how computers make shopping without cash possible. The customer gives the assistant a special card, which probably looks like an ordinary credit card. This card is fed into a computer terminal, which has replaced the old cash-register. This debits the customer's bank account by the amount of the goods purchased and simultaneously credits the store's account.

store's bank

customer's bank

+$45.20

−$45.20

store's computer

salesperson

computer terminal

customer

and one British bank is experimenting with systems such as this for paying for gasoline at gas stations.

Since there are already systems that bring access to a computer into every home, there is no reason why people should not find what they want to buy from the information provided by the computer system, then order and pay for the goods with the same system. We can already use the telephone to order and pay for goods by quoting a credit card number. Using a complete home shopping system is really only a very small step further than that.

Cash is still convenient for small purchases, but in the future, with the increasing availability of computerized money transactions, even cash may be unnecessary.

A device such as this small keyboard allows people to shop by telephone from home even more conveniently. The user dials the computer's number, and the computer answers with a high-pitched tone. The customer then taps on the keyboard the catalog number, the code number of the goods and the desired quantity, and his or her own account number; the keyboard transmits each of them into tones the computer recognizes and can convert into bits to process the order.

The End of Paper?

Computers in the future are likely to alter completely the presentation of the written word.

Compare the costs of keeping text on a computer to printing it on paper. A single magnetic tape costs as little as $15, it can hold millions of characters of data, and that data can be displayed within seconds as text on a screen. To store the same data in book form would cost hundreds of dollars and it would take minutes or even hours to find the relevant page or even the correct book. Of course, a whole computer system is needed to get the text on tape, and a VDU is needed to read it. But with the cost of computers halving every few years, the economic advantages of computers seem very strong. In ten or twenty years' time a good deal of material now in books may no longer be reproduced solely in book form. Almost every home may have television/computer terminals. People will be able to read books on their television screens, and they may be able to view newspapers on TV too.

Another advantage of keeping the printed word in computer storage is the space that can be saved. The texts of the nineteen million books in the Library of Congress could be fitted onto about thirty-five mass storage devices. Furthermore, one copy of a text stored on a computer could be viewed simultaneously by thousands of people throughout the world using VDUs linked to a computer network.

Computers are also replacing the written word in offices. A network of computers is used to provide

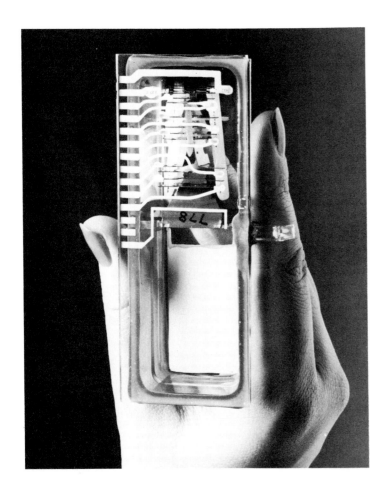

The recently developed flat screen television (above) has a unique screen (left), known as a liquid crystal display (LCD) screen. It measures only four by two by three-quarters of an inch. Televisions like this are portable, and any printed words – such as viewdata – are legible on them. Large, wall-mounted flat screen televisions are likely to be produced in the near future.

an electronic mail service between buildings and departments. Messages typed into one terminal can be sent to another terminal within seconds. In fact, we are just about to enter the age of the computerized office, which will take over from the present paper office. In some offices the computerized word processor has already made many typewriters obsolete. In the future, letters may be typed onto a word processor's keyboard and stored on magnetic disks. Any error seen on the screen can be corrected simply by using the keyboard, and paragraphs can be moved around and any phrases inserted. The system can also justify type, that is, make sure the right-hand margins are even, as in this book. The computer can change the line width and page depth, and even check the spelling. Once the letter is in the correct form it is stored and as many copies as required can be printed off, or sent to another screen, or even another computer.

Text on a computer can be very easy to find. If the

Journalists use computer terminals to prepare newspaper articles. They type the articles on a VDU, on which they can inspect and edit the text.

reader knows what he or she wants, the computer can locate and display the information within seconds. There are also programs that help people find documents if they are unsure what they are looking for. For example, a university might keep copies of research papers on a computer. A student wanting to learn about the life cycle of a worm would use the terminal to find out how many papers there are on worms, then narrow the subject down to the life cycle of the worm until the appropriate papers are found. The student can then inspect the papers on the VDU screen.

The Vanishing Computer?

Although the last thirty years have seen the rise of the computer from a scientific experiment to a machine of immense influence and usefulness, some people believe that in another thirty years computers will be a thing of the past.

A few years ago a factory machine could be controlled automatically by connecting it to a computer. The computer was a separate machine, possibly in another room. Now, some factory machines are not connected to a separate computer. Instead the machine itself includes a microprocessor. The computer does not control the machine, as every machine – whether it be a factory machine, a washing machine, or an automobile – includes its own data processing power; it is more or less intelligent in its own right. The computer, as a microprocessor, will disappear into the machine it controls. This is like using batteries to provide electric power. The batteries in a flashlight are not a separate electric power machine; they are part of the flashlight.

Computer power is also being distributed in another way. Instead of using one large computer, processing is starting to spread throughout organizations. Imagine a large supermarket chain. It uses a computerized cash register at each check-out. All the cash registers are connected to a single central controller in the store. The controllers for each store in the chain are all connected to a large central computer at the head office.

Each morning the controller for a store is given all the prices of the goods sold in its own store. When a customer comes to pay, the check-out clerk either keys in to the cash register code numbers for the goods that the customer has bought or, if the goods have the appropriate magnetic labels, passes the goods over a special sensing device that is attached to the cash register which records what they are. The cash register then gets the price of each item from the controller, adds up the customer's bill, prints it, and sends the total back to the controller. The cash register also gives the controller the overall totals for sales of particular categories of product.

When a cashier passes purchases over a laser scanner (left) that is connected to a cash register, bar codes (such as the one below) on the purchases are converted into numbers that are passed to the in-store computer. The computer passes back prices to the cash register and also updates the total quantity the store has in stock of the item purchased.

5 012345 678900

The keys on the cash register are color-coded, each color representing a particular category of product. The cashier enters the color for an appropriate item, clothes and accessories in this case, and also punches a key that records the price of that particular purchase. Each cash register in the store is linked to a central computer, which is also used for updating prices and categories and doing stock control.

The controller keeps these totals of the amounts spent on each category of product during the day, and a grand total of all the money spent in the store. Each controller passes this data to the central computer at the end of the day. So there is some data processing at the ten cash registers, some at the controller in each branch, and some at the computer at head office. In this way the data processing power is distributed all over the organization instead of being in one computer. This is known as distributed data processing.

A possible extension to this distributed data processing is based on viewdata, which enables anyone with the appropriate television set and a telephone to get access to vast quantities of information. But there is no reason why all the other services computers provide should not be available as part of the telephone service. In this case anyone who wants to use a computer, for example a scientist, a businessman, or someone in their own home, need not have a computer of their own because they can use a terminal connected to an ordinary telephone. In fact they do not need to know about computers at all because it is the telephone that provides them with the data processing service that will perform calculations, do accounts, store recipes and so on. In the future there may be very few computers as machines on their own. All the services that we now get from computers may be provided either by a microprocessor in another machine or as a public service through the telephone network.

The End of Commuting?

Most people travel to work every day. As cities grow larger, more and more people have to travel greater distances to get to work. This result is more commuting and worse rush hours. The computer may slow or reverse that trend. In the future, many people may be able to work at home most of the time, saving the drudgery and cost of commuting.

One reason people travel to work is because they need information that is available only at their offices: files, accounts, and so on. All this can be available at home through a computer terminal. Another important reason people go to an office or a factory to work is so that they can communicate conveniently with other people in the same organization.

The telephone already makes it possible to contact people who are miles away, but it is not good enough on its own to let most of us work at home. Several systems have been developed on which the speaker can see the other person on a screen as well as talk to him. It is also possible to send clear and accurate drawings and pictures over telephone lines. Computerized telephone exchanges make it possible to dial an extension in a large building from outside without having to be connected by the operator of the building's private exchange. If there is no reply, the telephone will automatically switch to another number that sends a radio wave to set off a bleeper. It is thus possible to contact people wherever they are in the building. Computers also allow a short written message to be sent almost instantaneously to other terminals.

In an office one person often needs to be able to communicate with many other people. Teleconferences enable several people to join in one telephone conversation at once, and the participants can leave the conversation and return to it as they please. All the people involved could be in different countries or even different continents.

You can imagine a company of the future, which might be based on a large central computer with a small staff to run it and practically everyone else working at home. Salesmen can get orders by telephone or terminals at home, and they can even

Commuting traffic comes to a halt outside Frankfurt in West Germany. Computers could make such a difference to our working lives that traveling to work becomes a far less common event in the future.

send sales literature by using telecopiers that relay pictures along telephone lines. They can send orders through their terminals to the company's central computer. Factories and warehouses will be almost totally automatic, with computerized robots operating machines. There are already warehouses that do not need any human intervention, as a computer keeps track of all the goods. When new goods arrive the computer tells a robot where to put them and when there is an order it instructs the robot to bring the appropriate goods to the dispatch bay. It also reminds the administrative staff to order new supplies when stocks are running low.

The computer is responsible for recording all sales, purchases, wages, and the other information on which the company depends. This means that all the information the management needs to run the company is available on the computer and can be inspected from terminals at home. Management can use the computer to find out what is going on, and use audio-visual systems to talk to other members of the staff. Any outsiders who want to contact the company could telephone a number and be directed automatically to the terminal at the home of the person who handles inquiries.

Of course, there will still be people who will have to travel to work. Many salesmen might not be effective or happy selling unless personally present, and there are certain jobs, such as construction, farming, police work, which could not possibly be done via any telephone line. However, for some of the working population commuting could become one of the agonies of the bad old days.

A two-way simultaneous video teleconference enables these seven people to communicate with colleagues at a center many miles away. Voice-activated cameras concealed in a screen zoom in on the person speaking. The man at the blackboard, who is also seen on the right-hand screen, is talking to the two people shown on the left-hand screen.

Can Computers Replace People?

Most people's jobs are likely to be affected by computers in one way or another. Teachers, for example, can use terminals in the classroom. Each pupil may one day have a terminal to use which can pose problems and ask questions, and the computer can inspect and check the pupil's replies. But could a computer ever replace teachers or do any job a man or woman can do? The short answer is that this is very unlikely.

At the moment there are vast numbers of things a computer cannot do. Computers cannot perform surgery or dock a supertanker. But they can help the people who do these tasks. In fact, computers can help nearly everyone, from an architect to a postal clerk. However, there is no program that makes a computer behave in anything like the way a human mind works. Even so, some people are trying to program computers to think like people. They have had some amazing successes. Some computer programs can play chess much better than the average player, and there is one game in which a computer has beaten the world champion: backgammon.

But playing backgammon is only one skill. How can we decide if a computer is as "intelligent" as a human being? A simple test has been suggested. The test involves two people who have never met before – person A and person B – and a computer, all three in separate rooms. A has to try to tell the

Many schools have taken advantage of the increasing availability of computers to introduce them into the classroom. These children are using the keyboard in the foreground to find out just what their school computer can do.

difference between B and the computer. B tries to make it clear to A that he is not a computer, but the computer is programmed to try to deceive A into thinking that it is B. Obviously A could tell easily if he could see into the other rooms, or if he could speak to B, so the only way that he can communicate with both the computer and B is through terminals. A has two terminals, one leading to each of the other rooms, and he can use them to ask any questions he likes. If he cannot tell from the replies which terminal leads to the computer, then it is generally accepted that the computer must be regarded as being as intelligent as a human. At the moment no program has been written which gets a computer anywhere near it.

Computers are only effective when problems are clearly defined in advance. They are next to useless when problems are not well defined. For example, an airplane can fly automatically most of the time, but there is always a human pilot in case something goes wrong. The human can react to any situation, some of which he may never have imagined. At the moment most computer programs need to know everything that might happen in advance, and what to do if it does happen. Such programs can be written if the computer is only playing backgammon, but they cannot be written for a nurse, an athlete, or any number of other professions.

Some people say that computers can never have "minds of their own" because they need a program, which is created by a human, to tell them what to do. This is perfectly true. But how do we know that a program cannot be written which gives a computer a mind of its own? A programmer cannot always predict how a computer running his or her program will react. There are many examples of a computer running a chess-playing program in which the computer has made the best possible choice of the alternative moves it was programmed to make. Despite this, it will be many years before a program is devised that is anything like the human mind.

Six chess experts, including International Master David Levy (center) and Grandmaster Michael Stean (second from left), challenge the computer. Each player in turn keys his move onto the keyboard and it is then shown on the screen. Next the computer makes its own move which is also shown on the screen. The second player reprograms the computer for the next move in the game he is playing with the computer, and so on. Of course, the computer can play against one person as well as several, and it can also be programmed for different levels of play – normal, aggressive, or passive.

More Data, More Quickly

When something changes by doubling during a specific period it is said to change exponentially. That is what computers are doing – every few years or so computers become twice as effective as they were before. In a hundred years' time exponential growth would mean that just a few chips could store about a billion characters – almost enough to hold one copy of the thirty-volume *Encyclopedia Britannica*, each of which contains forty-three million words. It is impossible to say what we would do with all this computer power. Computers are often used for things no one ever dreamed of previously, and there is no lack of demand so far. But can computers continue to change exponentially?

Perhaps computers will be limited because we will run out of the resources to make them. But computers become more powerful at the same time as they are getting smaller. Early computers occupied a whole room and more; a computer of equivalent power nowadays would fit on top of a desk. A chip that holds 64,000 bits today held only 4000 bits in 1973 (and the silicon from which the chips are made is the commonest element in the earth's crust after oxygen).

There are some limits, however. The basic law of physics relating the speed at which a circuit can be operated to the electric power needed to do so is an example. In the end it will not be possible to operate conventional circuits any more quickly without increasing the power so much that they melt. But, at the moment, silicon, which has a melting point of 2552°F, is used only at temperatures of 77–80°F, so that limit is a long way from being reached.

At the moment the silicon chip is supreme for circuits, and it will take us a lot further. If it should fail to keep up the pace there are plenty of alternatives waiting to take over. There is the Josephson junction and there is another kind of chip made from a substance called gallium arsenide instead of silicon. The advantage in this material is that electricity can move more quickly through gallium arsenide than it can through silicon.

All these kinds of chip are based on electricity, but there is no reason why computers should always be electric. Research is being conducted into using light in the form of laser beams instead of electricity. The bits are recorded as the presence or absence of a particular wavelength of light in a beam. The problem with using light to carry the bits is to find an equivalent to the transistor, some kind of switch that can be turned on or off. Recent research suggests that it may be possible to change the wavelength of a beam so that it can act like a switch.

Whatever they are made of, there are many other ways in which computers can become more powerful. It is not just the basic building-blocks of the devices that matter, it is how they are organized. Most computers at the moment bring each item of data, one at a time, to the instructions in the processor. But research is also being done to enable the computer to work on different instructions – adding and subtracting, for example – simultaneously.

Although the organization is just as important as the basic devices, the software in any computer system is even more important. People in the computing industry want to use computers in many ways, and while computers have the power for these different uses there are not enough programmers to write the programs. In one effort to solve this problem, newer and better computer languages are continually being developed. There are some that enable a scientist to write an instruction in one statement which would take ten or twenty statements in FORTRAN. An instruction to find the highest number in a group of numbers, for example, can be made in one statement in APL (*A Programming Language*), whereas it would need many more statements to achieve the same instruction in most other languages. It is new software, and new ways of writing it, that will probably have the greatest effect of all on the power of future computers.

Computers for the future: specific details of the scene shown on the small VDU screen at left are flashed up on the large screen in the background by touching the VDU screen, which is sensitive to the finger's warmth.

Glossary

Adder: a group of switches, usually on silicon chips, that adds two binary numbers together.

Address: a number assigned to a main storage location at the time a computer is manufactured. All computer programs refer to locations by this number to obtain the data contained there.

Arithmetic/logic unit: the part of the processor that carries out the instructions of a program.

Binary: a numeric system that uses only the two digits zero and one, as compared to the decimal system, which uses ten digits – zero through nine.

Bit: a condensed form of the two words "binary dig*it*." The two binary digits are zero and one and all data in a computer is coded as a combination of these two symbols.

Branch: a computer instruction that makes the processor break the normal sequence of instructions to start working on a different set of instructions.

Byte: a group of eight bits, normally enough to hold one character of English.

Capacitor: an electronic component that can store an electric charge and is used in main storage. A charged capacitor holds a one bit, an uncharged capacitor holds a zero bit (or vice versa).

Chip: a tiny piece of silicon in which are embedded microscopic electronic circuits.

Code: the combination of bits used to represent every letter and number.

Compiler: a computer program that translates programs from the language in which they were originally written into bits.

Conductor: any substance, such as copper, that will conduct electricity. Conductors are essential for all computers.

Control unit: the part of the processor that reads the next instruction from main storage and directs it either to the arithmetic/logic unit or to another device.

Data: the information used by a computer.

Disk drive: the part of the computer system that contains the read/write head, which reads from and writes onto a magnetic disk.

Disk pack: a group of magnetic disks sharing a common spindle.

External storage: any kind of computer storage, such as magnetic disks, other than main storage.

Firmware: a program permanently stored in a special part of the processor whose instructions are used by all other programs in the computer. Because this program cannot be changed or removed from the computer it is halfway between software and hardware.

Hardware: the machines that make up a computer system.

Input device: a machine that converts into bits the data received from some source outside the computer.

Insulator: any substance, such as rubber, that prevents electricity from flowing through it.

Josephson junction: a new type of very fast electronic circuit that may be used to store and process data; it could replace the silicon chip in the future.

Language: the specialized words and phrases other than bits that are devised to simplify writing computer programs. The computer has to translate the languages into bits before it can process them.

Laser beam: a highly concentrated beam of light, used in a variety of ways in some computers.

Line printer: an output device that prints a line of type at a time.

Location: the smallest part of main storage, which holds one item of data and has its own address.

Loop: a group of instructions in a program that is repeated many times.

Magnetic disk: one of the most popular forms of external storage, consisting of a disk of magnetic material that stores data in the form of magnetic marks.

Magnetic tape: the cheapest form of external storage, which holds data as magnetic marks on the tape.

Main storage: the central storage device in any computer system. All data passes through main storage on its way from one device to another, and all the instructions in a computer program must be in main storage before they can be obeyed.

Mass storage device: a device that can store large quantities of data on magnetic rolls, which work in a similar way to magnetic tape.

Microcomputer: a small computer that uses a microprocessor.

Microprocessor: a complete computer processor on one silicon chip.

Minicomputer: a small computer, larger than a microcomputer, that is often dedicated to only one task.

Not gate: a group of switches that turns a zero bit into a one bit and vice versa.

Operating system: the program that is permanently in main storage, reading in and supervising all the other programs. The computer manufacturer normally provides the operating system.

Output device: a machine that converts the bits inside the computer to a form, such as punched cards, that can be used outside the computer.

Processor: the device that works on, or processes, data.

Program: the set of instructions that tells the computer what to do with the data it processes.

Punched cards: stiff paper cards in which holes representing data are punched; the computer converts the holes in the cards into data on a card reader.

Random access memory: the most common form of main storage, made from hundreds of thousands of microscopic capacitors and transistors embedded in a silicon chip.

Read/write head: the part of a disk or tape drive that reads and writes data from and onto the disk or tape.

Silicon: the material from which chips are made.

Software: strictly, the programs sold by the manufacturers with their computers, although often applied to all programs.

Tape drive: the device that contains the read/write head, which reads from and writes onto magnetic tape.

Terminal: an input and output device that can give information to the computer and also receive information from it very quickly.

Track: parallel lines on magnetic disks and tapes.

Transistor: an electronic component that allows a current to pass or not. Most computer switches are now made from transistors engraved onto chips.

Virtual storage: a means of using disks to enable programs to use main storage more efficiently.

Visual display unit: a computer input and output device on which input is a keyboard and output is a screen.

Word: a unit of storage, larger than a byte, composed of enough bits to store most numbers in the binary system. The size of a word varies from one computer to another.

Index

Credits

The Publishers gratefully acknowledge permission to reproduce the following illustrations:

American Telephone and Telegraph Company 89; Black Star 43, 90; BOC Datasolve Ltd 32; Paul Brierley 31, 51, 64, 67r, 73b; The British Piano Museum, Charitable Trust 17; British Telecom 48r, 73t, 78; Control Data Ltd. 9tl; Ian Cooper 15b, 72; Daily Telegraph Colour Library 47, 83; Roger di Vito 16; EMI Ltd 9bl; Express & Star Ltd 85; Ferranti Ltd 52l; Courtesy of Honeywell 39; IBM 44, 48, 67l, 69; ICL 37r, 57; The Image Bank 3, 50, 63, 71; Iseki Poly-Tech – Photo: Peirs Harding/Tunnels & Tunnelling 9r; Lufthansa German Airlines 45; Robert Mohl 93; NCR Ltd 86l, 87; Pictor International 8; Securitas Ltd 81r; Science Photo Library 27, 30, 65, 68, 80; Science Research Council 70; Sinclair Research Ltd 84; Space Frontiers Ltd 55, 75; Texas Instruments Inc. 91; Trewin Copplestone Books Ltd 42 (John Sims), 58, 60; ZEFA Picture Library (UK) Ltd 36, 88.

Cover photograph: Oxford Scientific Films Ltd

Artwork by Hayward and Martin

Bibliography

The Computer Revolution, Nigel Hawkes; E. P. Dutton, 1971
The Computerized Society, James Martin and Adrian R. D. Norman; Prentice-Hall, 1970
Electronic Computers, Hollindale and Tooting; Penguin Books, 1965
Illustrating BASIC, Donald Alcock; Cambridge University Press, 1977
The Micro Revolution, Peter Laurie; Futura, 1980
Microelectronics, A Scientific American Publication, 1977
The Mighty Micro, Christopher Evans; Viking Press, 1980
The Mind Tool, Neill Graham; West Publishing Company, 1980
The Personal Computer Book, Robin Bradbeer; Gower Publications, 1980